The ABCs of
Collecting Online 2

How to Buy, Sell Antiques & Collectibles on the Internet

Published by Hobby House Press
Grantsville, Maryland 21536

Dedication

To my mother Helen, my children Danielle and Nicolas, my late grandmother Stella who started me down this path, and for my wife Carolyn and our best friend Annie, who together have pursued a lifelong dedication to collecting that was the inspiration for this book.

ABC's of Collecting Online has been written to be as accurate as possible. The author, publisher, agents and assignees cannot be held responsible for any error that may occur within the text of this book, nor held responsible for any problems or cumputer viruses that the user may encounter utilizing the Internet or any other online service provider.

Ray Boileau has been involved in the pre-press and printing industry for twenty-five years and was among the first in the 1970s to experiment with computers as a complement to printing, long before desktop publishing was conceived. He currently is a computer consultant who designs Web pages and specializes in Web site implementation.

Ray has also been buying and selling antiques and collectibles for eighteen years. He now works as an antiques dealer offering Internet sales as well as selling through several conventional locations. He has been using or monitoring many of the online auctions since their inceptions.

Photo - Title Page and Back Cover: A Nippon Raised Relief Humidor with green wreath mark. Internet bidding for this item reached $800.00.

Additional copies of this book may be purchased at $12.95 (plus postage and handling) from
Hobby House Press, Inc.
1 Corporate Drive
Grantsville, Maryland 21536
1-800-554-1447
or from your favorite bookstore or dealer.
ISBN: 0-87588-559-4

TABLE OF CONTENTS

Introduction

As we approach the new millenium, the significance of our past is amplified with each day that passes. The speed with which our world moves today has made us all, at one time or another, think about what we perceive as "simpler times." Baby boomers long for the toys of their youth. Doll collectors yearn for the Bru that twenty years ago they could afford and now cannot. Furniture enthusiasts bemoan the fact that the oldest and best examples have found their way into museums and private collections, and have all but disappeared from the marketplace. What's left to collect?

Everything and anything! Most of us have a natural instinct to collect. Perhaps your grandmother gave you a piece of depression glass, as mine did years ago, and after some study you discovered that there were many more pieces in her pattern available. I now have an extensive collection of yellow Florentine #2 depression glass because it reminds me of someone I respected, admired, and miss greatly.

Maybe as a child you started off to school each day with your Roy Rogers lunchbox and, in inclement weather, your Roy Rogers rain slicker. Wouldn't it be fun to own them again?

Your collecting fancy doesn't even have to be for older things. Beanie Babies and Pokémon are perfect examples of collectibles introduced quite recently that have gained immediate popularity. The Gene® doll, introduced in 1995 by Ashton-Drake, has captured the imagination of doll collectors who want to play with their dolls, not leave them in boxes on a shelf. There is already a secondary market for these recently introduced collectibles, with some items selling for hundreds and even thousands of dollars more than they cost just a few years ago.

That being said, I urge you to not get caught up in the "collecting for profit" trap unless you're a dealer and your livelihood comes from buying and selling. For every story of somebody paying $25.00 for a piece of Roseville pottery in the morning and selling it for $250.00 that same afternoon, there are thousands of disappointing stories you won't hear. Even experienced dealers don't always get it right when buying for profit. I once bought an oak lady's desk at an auction for $180.00 and after displaying it in three different locations over 18 months settled for an offer of $200.00 to get it sold. Yes, it sold for $20 more than I paid. But when you factor in the costs associated with maintaining a shop or mall booth it was a definite loss. And I won't even mention the "bargains" I have sold on the Internet without a reserve—so sure they would sell for much more than I paid and so disappointed when I didn't even break even. Collecting for pleasure is much less painful!

In the past, collections were built over time. Amassing a sizeable collection required visiting antique malls, flea markets, yard sales, auctions...in short, logging a lot of miles. Most collectors didn't have the time or money it required to travel the entire country searching for that one elusive piece, and settled for buying trips within a few hours drive from home.

Today, the Internet has opened a vast market that you can access from your library or den. Collections that used to take a lifetime to acquire can now be completed in a few weeks, if you're willing to spend the money that quickly. The rules have changed, and you need to change with them to take full advantage of the possibilities.

Most of you probably have already heard of eBay™, even if you ve never been on the Internet. Started in late 1995 as a place for collectors to buy, sell and trade, it quickly became the model for a multitude of online auctions that have sprung up all over cyberspace. eBay™ has been through growing pains, with frequent outages as their user base grew to enormous proportions. Recently they announced a controversial reserve price policy, assessing a fee for setting a reserve on your item and dictating where you must start your opening bid when you set a reserve. This practice has alienated some members who have started to look for alternative places to do business.

For a long time, eBay™ was the only game in town. Now there are hundreds of Internet auction sites, but none has so much as dented eBay's™ dominance of the marketplace. Several new sites that launched during 1998 have already expired in 1999, and the ones that have survived do not seem to be flourishing. Amazon.com was expected to give eBay™ a run for their money when they launched their auction business. Although Amazon.com has made a strong showing compared to others, so far it is not a serious challenger.

So formidable is eBay™ s grip that on September 17, 1999 a privately held company, FairMarket, announced they were creating a network designed to link smaller auction sites in order to achieve the critical mass required to compete with eBay™. Members so far include Microsoft, Excite, Ticketmaster, CBS Sportsline, Lycos, Dell, CompUSA, Xoom.com, Tripod, and Ziff-Davis with more members planned. In essence what will happen is that listings posted on Excite auctions will appear on the auction sites of the other members as well. This will make for some interesting "partners," such as when Dell Computer auctions appear on the Microsoft site.

What impact the FairMarket Auction Network(sm) will have remains to be seen. The only thing that seems sure is that the Internet is already beginning to enter the merger and acquisitions stage of its existence, spelling disaster once again for the "little guy." Just as the corner grocery store is now mostly a memory, so in the future will be online auction sites that do not form a network or alliance with a larger group. This is somewhat disturbing, as the Internet has been touted as a way for small business to achieve equal footing with the big boys. At least in the world of online auctions, this is simply not so.

Since you're reading this book, you've probably already got the collecting bug. If you don't have it, keep reading and then experience the online auctions. I'm betting you'll be hooked. We all like to collect something—even your house collects dust!

A Victorian metal statuette with a wooden base found online.

An Indian decorative mask
by artist Michelle Malpica
of Isinglass Studios.

A Buffalo Pottery
Deldane Humidor
purchased for $237.00
at www.cyrbid.com.

CHAPTER 1
Welcome to the Future!

The Internet is here to stay, and the faster you get on board the better. Not only that, it is maturing at an alarming rate. As a testament to the worldwide credibility of the Internet one need look no further than the date of September 11, 1998 when it was used as the main vehicle to disseminate information about the relationship between President William Jefferson Clinton and Monica Lewinsky. On that day some Web sites recorded over 300,000 hits each hour as the world scrambled for a look at the Starr Report submitted to Congress only a few days before. As one of the most important news stories in 25 years unfolded, the Internet was the information source, and marked its passing into adolescence.

To have access to this powerful medium you need only a computer with a keyboard and monitor, a modem, browser software (usually provided with new computer purchases), a phone line, the money to pay your monthly access fee, and a willingness to learn. When these conditions are satisfied you become one of millions of computers networked to the World Wide Web, thus forming the Internet. Once there you will marvel at the ease of navigation provided by hyperlinks and search engines. You will be astounded at the sheer volume of antiques and collectibles that are suddenly available for purchase, and you will become a member of a global community. Your life will be changed forever.

The U.S. military originally conceived what today is known as the Internet as a way of keeping communications open in time of national emergency. In the late 1960s the Defense Department commissioned the Advanced Research Projects Agency (ARPA) to devise a system of communications, using computers, that could be rerouted in the event that main lines were destroyed or tampered with. This network came to be known as ARPANET and, in the beginning, was difficult to use in contrast to today's user-friendliness.

Next to recognize the importance of interconnected domains was the academic community. In searching for a way to quickly distribute information among themselves and their universities, the National Science Foundation began forming their own network that was dubbed NSFNET in it's honor. NSFNET was built during the 1980s and eventually connected with the military network, with the result being the beginnings of the Internet we know today.

Internet Access

The route most people take to the Internet is their home telephone line. Other avenues are available, such as access over cable TV lines, ISDN or T-1 lines, and satellite connections. These other types of Internet access provide faster throughput of data but are more expensive than using existing phone lines. The average user, including home office workers and small businesses, can get by readily with a phone line connection. The casual user may want to investigate WebTV, which utilizes a VCR-like box that sits on top of your television set and affords you Internet access via your TV screen. This is the least expensive way to get to the Internet, but is also the most limiting in terms of visual resolution. You need a keyboard with WebTV if you want to interact; otherwise you can only watch as the Internet passes you by.

Your Window to the World

Computer users need software aptly called a browser to open the window and let the Internet in. Netscape Navigator and Microsoft's Internet Explorer are the two most commonly used. Both browsers are good, and I don't recommend one over the other. You'll probably end up using the one a friend recommends, the one that is already installed on your computer, or the one that you get your hands on first. Browsers are started, or launched, the same way most other programs on your computer are, from the Start—Programs menu if you are using Windows 95 or 98, or from a shortcut icon on your desktop.

Addresses

Once your window to the world is open, how do you *point your browser* where you want it to go? By using an address, known in Internet lingo as a URL (Uniform Resource Locator). Every resource on the World Wide Web has it's own unique URL. URL is pronounced one letter at a time just as you see it: U-R-L. If you refer to it by pronouncing a word that rhymes with girl you will be identifying yourself as a novice, and we wouldn't want that, would we?

The majority of documents you view online are created in *hypertext markup language* (html) which is currently the standard language of the Internet. This language allows the linking abilities that make navigating the Internet so interesting. By simply clicking on a hypertext link you are whisked to another part of the document you are viewing, or perhaps to a completely new document which contains further information about the link you just clicked on.

Most Internet addresses take the form **http://www.servername.xxx** where http:// stands for *hypertext transfer protocol* (note that the :// after http MUST be used and the slashes must be the forward, and not backward, slashes), www stands for *world wide web*, servername is the name an Internet Service Provider uses to identify their host computer, and xxx is an abbreviation for the type of *domain* the address is using. The different parts are separated by a period, pronounced "dot" when reciting the address. Abbreviations for U.S. domains are as follows...

com	Business and Commercial
edu	Educational Institutions
gov	Government Institutions
mil	Military Installations
net	Network Resources
org	Other organizations

Web Sites and Web Pages

A *Web page* can be as simple as a paragraph of text or as complex as a combination of text, animated graphics, and audio and video clips. Most Web pages have *hyperlinks*, which appear as different colored and/or underlined text, or sometimes as a colored box around a graphic. When you pass your cursor over a hyperlink the arrow changes to a hand with a finger pointing up. When you click on a hyperlink you are whisked to a different part of the Web page you are viewing or possibly to another Web page entirely. A group of Web pages that are designed to be viewed together, one at a time, using hyperlinks, is called a *Web site*.

Search Engines

The fastest way to find Web sites related to a particular topic is by using a *search engine*. A search engine allows you to type in a word or words, known as *keywords*, that you are seeking information about and it then "searches" the Internet for Web sites that contain those words. What actually happens is that the search engines are constantly monitoring the Internet with programs referred to as *robots*. Information is collected and indexed in database form, readily available to answer inquiries. Otherwise a search of the Internet would take much longer than any of us is willing to wait.

There are options for narrowing your search if the engine returns too many sites (which it often does) or you can run a new search adding or omitting some of your keywords. The search engine will return a page or pages of hyperlinks with brief descriptions of the Web site that you simply click on to go to that site.

Be aware that all search engines are not created equal; that's one reason there is more than one of them. Each search engine provider hopes that their product will be the most comprehensive at finding quality Web sites to match your search parameters. Realistically the World Wide Web is a huge place and the technology available today just doesn't allow a single search engine to find everything—it is estimated that even the best search engines are capable of indexing less than 20% of the entire Internet. Therefore, should you not find any matches for your search with, say, the *AltaVista™* search engine, try *Yahoo!*, *Webcrawler™* and several others before abandoning your quest.

You can type more than one word when using a search engine and it will search for Web sites containing all of the words. If you want to search for a string of words that must fall together exactly as you type them, enclose them in quotes. For example, a search of the AltaVista™ search engine yielded the following results . . .

A search for the word **dolls** returned 488,921 sites.

A search for the words **modern dolls**, without quotes, returned 797,830 sites. In this case the search engine is looking for sites that contain both of the keywords anywhere on the site.

A search for the words **"modern dolls"**, with quotes, returned 771 sites, because the search found only sites that used the keywords in the exact order they were typed.

In contrast, here are the results of the same searches on the Webcrawler™ search engine . . .

A search for the word **dolls** returned 5273 sites.

A search for the words **modern dolls**, without quotes, returned 36,529 sites.

A search for the words **"modern dolls"**, with quotes, returned 26 sites.

As mentioned before, it is good to get familiar with several search engines, as they will return different results. In our example above, AltaVista™ returned many more sites, in fact too many to explore without narrowing the field. Statistics show that most people will look no further than the first 10 entries returned by a search engine before moving on. Even with all of those choices, you might find the exact site you are looking for in the Webcrawler™ results instead, so remember to explore when your first search comes up empty!

If a search engine returns hyperlinks with a percentage in front of each one, that percentage represents how much of your search string was found on that particular page. Obviously you should visit the highest percentage pages first.

To help get you started, here are the URLs of my favorite search engines. Once you get the hang of using them you can use these search engines to search for other search engines!

www.altavista.digital.com
www.excite.com
www.hotbot.com
www.infoseek.com
www.lycos.com
www.webcrawler.com
www.yahoo.com

When you visit these search engine sites, I would recommend that you *bookmark* them for future use. Bookmarking is simply adding them to the *Favorites* menu of your browser, allowing you to return to the site with a single click from that point on.

Your browser will probably have both a menu and a toolbar button for Favorites—they perform similar functions. The menu categories go across the very top of the browser window, and the toolbar buttons are below it.

Go to the **Favorites** menu of your browser and click **Add To Favorites**. Depending on which browser you use, and which operating system resides on your computer, you will get a message asking if you want to subscribe to the page or something similar. Windows 98 users will simply get a dialog box saying that Internet Explorer will add the page to your favorites list. If you get the message asking if you want to subscribe to a page select **No, Just Add to Favorites** and then click **OK**. Windows 98 users can simply click **OK**. Note also that you can arrange your favorites into folders for easy access later. For instance, you can create a folder for search engines and one for online auctions so you don't have to look through sites for both when wanting to visit again.

From that point on, by clicking the Favorites button on the toolbar you will see a list of sites you have bookmarked. If you organize your favorite sites into folders you will see the folders and must click on the appropriate one to open it. Click once on any of the sites to be taken there immediately. If you're having problems or want to learn more, go to the Search feature of your browser's **Help** menu and type in *"favorite"* for additional information.

Netiquette

I would be remiss if I didn't mention something about the way to conduct yourself when online. There are a few "rules of the Internet highway" that you should know before communicating with the world.

1. Always remember you are a member of a community, and are responsible for your actions and particularly your words. Whether conversing via e-mail, posting an online auction listing or posting to a newsgroup you must never forget that you are interacting with people, not computers. People have emotions, so pay attention to your message.

2. Don't use capital letters when communicating via the Internet— it's considered the online equivalent of yelling.

3. Keep it brief! Verbosity will only bore and possibly anger the Internet community. Most Internet surfers are in a hurry and aren't online to read *War and Peace*.

4. When responding to someone else's message, quote what they said along with your answer. Many e-mail programs allow you to do this automatically—read the **Help** file of your program to see how to set the default to send messages with your replies.

5. Always remember that your private e-mail is not entirely private. It is possible for your messages to be intercepted by others, so you should never send private information (credit card numbers, etc.) without first learning about the encryption features of your e-mail program. Go to the **Help** menu of your e-mail program and search for the word **encrypt**. After reading and understanding the information, you can make an informed decision about whether you trust sending sensitive information this way. It is also a good policy to send credit card information in two separate e-mail messages, with each message containing one-half of the number. This practice greatly reduces the chance of someone being able to intercept it.

SEARCH ENGINES

altavista.digital.com

AltaVista ®
Connections

The most powerful and useful guide to the Net

September 20, 1999 PDT

My AltaVista Shopping.com Zip2.com

Ask AltaVista® a question. Or enter a few words in [any language ▼]

Help
Advanced Text Search

Search For: ⦿ Web Pages ○ Images ○ Video ○ Audio

[   ] [Search]

Search tip:
use audio search

Example: **Where can I find information about diseases?**

ALTAVISTA CHANNELS - My AltaVista - Finance - Travel - Shopping - Careers - Health - News - Entertainment

FREEACCESS - Download Software^New - Support **USEFUL TOOLS** - Family Filter - Translation - Yellow Pages - People Finder - Maps - Usenet - Free Email

DIRECTORY

Automotive

Business & Finance

Computers & Internet

Health & Fitness

Hobbies & Interests

Home & Family

Media & Amusements

People & Chat

Reference & Education

Shopping & Services

Society & Politics

Sports & Recreation

Travel & Vacations

OTHER TOOLS

▶ AltaVista Discovery 1.1
▶ Free Photo Albums
▶ Make us your Home Page
▶ Get Internet Explorer 5
▶ AV Tools & Gadgets
▶ Industrial Communities
▶ Search Products

ALTAVISTA HIGHLIGHTS

POWER SEARCH
▶ Search smart & enter for your chance to WIN $1000
    DAILY with the Universal Search for Knowledge!

NEW MEDIA NOW
▶ Take the Challenge: FREE Fantasy Football!
▶ Translate a web site with **AltaVista's Babel Fish**

ALTAVISTA NETWORK
▶ FREE Internet access! No fees, no time limits!
▶ Go local! Find a business near you fast

ULTRA SHOPPING FROM Shopping.com

Star Trek-Insurrection
Shopping.com Price: $21.99 You **Save:** $8.00

Pokemon Blue - Game Boy
Shopping.com Price: $25.99 You **Save:** $4.00

Quicken 2000 for Mac
Shopping.com Price: $59.95 You **Save:**

3Dfx Voodoo3 AGP 3D
Shopping.com Price: $215.95 You **Save:**

Click for more Ultra Shopping

NEWS BY ABCNEWS.com
▶ President Plans Storm Zone Tour
▶ Raisa Gorbachev Dies
▶ First Troops Arrive in East Timor
▶ Astronaut Nametag Auctioned for $310,500

Going...

FurnitureFind.com

TRY THESE SEARCHES...

Ryder Cup - campaign 2000 - health - Big 12 - Linux - celebrities

OUR SPONSORS

•Match.Com: The Best Site for Singles

•Click to Personalize with My AltaVista

•eWanted.com turns auctions upside down

•Click Here to Shop online at AltaVista!

ALTAVISTA INFORMATION
▶ International
▶ About AltaVista
▶ Job Openings
▶ Press Room

About AltaVista | Help | Feedback | Advertising Info | Add a Page

www.excite.com

Personalize Your Page!   Choose your favorite photo! »

New Members **Sign Up** • Excite Members **Sign In** • **Help**

My Excite
✉ **FREE Voicemail/Email**
📇 **Calendar/Address Book**
Free Excite Voicemail cool!

Today on Excite
Monday, September 20, 12:13PM EDT
News Raisa Gorbachev Dies
✗**Poll** Christians Targeted?
· Find a Cheap Ticket
· @Home Cable Net Access
· Excite Voicemail: Free!

Switch your **ISP today**!

| Search | More Search |

Autos   **Family**   **News**
Careers   **Games**   **Real Estate**
Computers **Health**   **Relationships**
Education **Lifestyle** **Sports**
Entertainment ! **Money** **Travel**

☐ **Hot! Excite College Clubs**

Shopping Auctions Classifieds Photo Gallery
Sensual Zone Horoscope Shop Catalogs Gadgets
More...

[People & Chat] Chat Now! 6809 People
Voice Chat Discussions Personals People Finder
More...

Shortcuts
FREE Voicemail
Stock Quotes
Yellow Pages
Airline Tickets
Movie Showtimes
Desktop Radio new!
Job Finder
Classifieds
Maps & Directions
Horoscopes
More...

2 minutes to **3.9% APR**!

My Stocks   edit _ X
Sponsored by **Charles Schwab**

| Get Quotes |

Full Portfolio		Alerts
Symbol	Price	Change
Nasdaq	2872.54	+2.92
Dow	10802.68	-0.95
S&P 500	1332.82	-2.60
ATHM	37.75	-0.69
INTU	104.12	+1.12

Open an account with Schwab
* = News Today H/L = 52 wk high/low
Last update Sep 20 12:13PM EDT
All data delayed at least 20 minutes
Most Active | Market Update
Full Portfolio | Symbol Lookup

My Sports   edit _ X
Monday
National Football League
Atlanta at   09:00 PM
Dallas   TV: ABC
Major League Baseball
Cleveland at   07:05 PM
Detroit   TV: local
Sports Home NFL MLB NHL NBA
College Football MLS Tennis Auto
Racing Golf Sports Boards FREE

My News   edit _ X
Top Stories | Photos (Sep 20 12:07PM)
· Cuba Jails U.S. Residents For Migrant Smuggling
· More Than 1,000 UN Troops Arrive In E.Timor
· Thousands Commemorate Victims Of Texas Shootings

ZDNet Tech News (Sep 18 6:45PM)
· Infoseek exec nabbed in sex scandal
· Jilted again! Amiga scraps PC plan
· What's next for Palm Computing?

Business News (Sep 20 12:05PM)
· U.S. Stocks Inch Higher; Tech Shares Gain
· Quaker Oats To Close Plants, Cut Jobs
· VoiceStream To Buy Aerial For

Sports News (Sep 20 11:49AM)
· Faxon Beats Funk In Playoff To Win B.C. Open
· Sosa, McGwire To Face Off At Wrigley Field
· Falcons' Chandler Doubtful Vs. Cowboys

More News...

My Weather   edit _ X
Enter your Zip Code:
| Submit |

[Airport Delays | 3D Weather]

My Services   edit _ X
· Buy Books at Amazon.com
· AT&T Communication Center
· Buy Software at Beyond.com
· Buy CDs at CDNOW.com
· Find a home with Realtor.com
· Reel.com, The Best Place to Buy Movies
· Shop at the Bank One Financial Center

My Chat   _ X
6809 **people chatting**
Billy Boat Indy race car driver
September 20 @10pm ET
Psychics & Astrologers Every weeknight @9pm ET
More Chat Events...

Message
Boards | Communities

www.hotbot.com

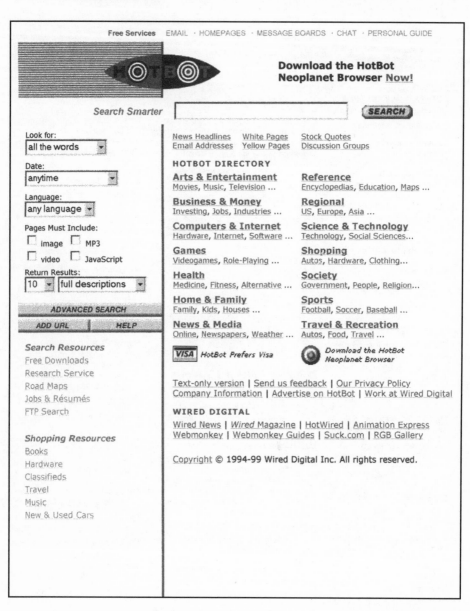

Free Services   EMAIL · HOMEPAGES · MESSAGE BOARDS · CHAT · PERSONAL GUIDE

**Download the HotBot
Neoplanet Browser Now!**

Search Smarter

SEARCH

Look for:
all the words

Date:
anytime

Language:
any language

Pages Must Include:
☐ image   ☐ MP3
☐ video   ☐ JavaScript

Return Results:
10   full descriptions

ADVANCED SEARCH

ADD URL   **HELP**

Search Resources
Free Downloads
Research Service
Road Maps
Jobs & Résumés
FTP Search

Shopping Resources
Books
Hardware
Classifieds
Travel
Music
New & Used Cars

News Headlines   White Pages   Stock Quotes
Email Addresses   Yellow Pages   Discussion Groups

HOTBOT DIRECTORY

Arts & Entertainment
Movies, Music, Television ...

Business & Money
Investing, Jobs, Industries ...

Computers & Internet
Hardware, Internet, Software ...

Games
Videogames, Role-Playing ...

Health
Medicine, Fitness, Alternative ...

Home & Family
Family, Kids, Houses ...

News & Media
Online, Newspapers, Weather ...

Reference
Encyclopedias, Education, Maps ...

Regional
US, Europe, Asia ...

Science & Technology
Technology, Social Sciences...

Shopping
Autos, Hardware, Clothing...

Society
Government, People, Religion...

Sports
Football, Soccer, Baseball ...

Travel & Recreation
Autos, Food, Travel ...

VISA *HotBot Prefers Visa*   *Download the HotBot Neoplanet Browser*

Text-only version | Send us feedback | Our Privacy Policy
Company Information | Advertise on HotBot | Work at Wired Digital

WIRED DIGITAL

Wired News | *Wired* Magazine | HotWired | Animation Express
Webmonkey | Webmonkey Guides | Suck.com | RGB Gallery

Copyright © 1994-99 Wired Digital Inc. All rights reserved.

www.infoseek.com

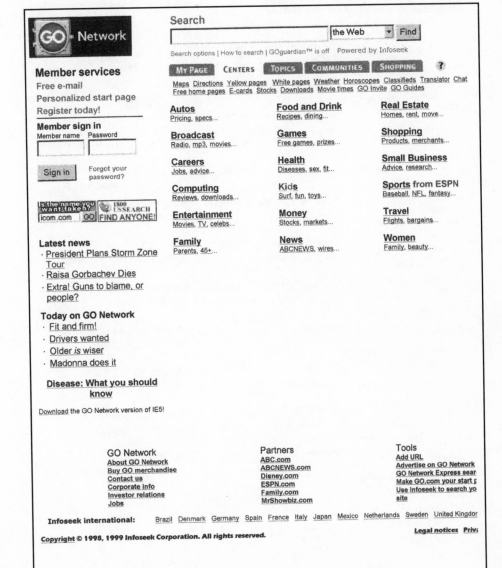

GO Network

Search

| the Web ▾ | Find |

Search options | How to search | GOguardian™ is off   Powered by Infoseek

MY PAGE **CENTERS** **TOPICS** **COMMUNITIES** **SHOPPING** **?**

Maps Directions Yellow pages White pages Weather Horoscopes Classifieds Translator Chat
Free home pages E-cards Stocks Downloads Movie times GO Invite GO Guides

Member services

Free e-mail
Personalized start page
Register today!

Member sign in

Member name   Password

Sign in   Forgot your
password?

Is the name you want taken?
icom .com GO **1800 US SEARCH FIND ANYONE!**

Latest news

· President Plans Storm Zone Tour
· Raisa Gorbachev Dies
· Extra! Guns to blame, or people?

Today on GO Network

· Fit and firm!
· Drivers wanted
· Older *is* wiser
· Madonna does it

Disease: What you should know

Download the GO Network version of IE5!

Autos
Pricing, specs...

Broadcast
Radio, mp3, movies...

Careers
Jobs, advice...

Computing
Reviews, downloads...

Entertainment
Movies, TV, celebs...

Family
Parents, 45+...

Food and Drink
Recipes, dining...

Games
Free games, prizes...

Health
Diseases, sex, fit...

Kids
Surf, fun, toys...

Money
Stocks, markets...

News
ABCNEWS, wires...

Real Estate
Homes, rent, move...

Shopping
Products, merchants...

Small Business
Advice, research...

Sports from ESPN
Baseball, NFL, fantasy...

Travel
Flights, bargains...

Women
Family, beauty...

GO Network
About GO Network
Buy GO merchandise
Contact us
Corporate info
Investor relations
Jobs

Partners
ABC.com
ABCNEWS.com
Disney.com
ESPN.com
Family.com
MrShowbiz.com

Tools
Add URL
Advertise on GO Network
GO Network Express sear
Make GO.com your start p
Use Infoseek to search yo
site

Infoseek international: Brazil Denmark Germany Spain France Italy Japan Mexico Netherlands Sweden United Kingdor

www.lycos.com

LYCOS NEWS
September 20, 1999

- Ft. Worth Funerals Begin
- Peace Force Bound For E. Timor
- Gators Defeat Vols, and NFL Week 2

More Lycos News...

SHOPPING

- New Stephen King Book 40% Off!
- 7¢ 7¢ 7¢ Long Distance
- Design & Print A Card At Home!

More Shopping...

ON LYCOS NOW

- Handspring, Football & Floyd: The Lycos 50
- Listen to the Best Music on Lycos Radio
- FIND ANYONE Right Now!

What's New...

Arts & Entertainment
Movies, TV, Music...

Business & Careers
Real Estate, Jobs, Investing...

Computers & Internet
Hardware, Software, Internet...

Games
Computer, Web, Video...

Health
Nutrition, Diseases, Fitness...

Home & Family
Kids, Recipes, Gardens...

News
Online, Media, Newspapers...

Recreation
Autos, Travel, Outdoors...

Reference
Education, Databases, Dictionaries...

Regional
US, Canada, Europe...

Science & Technology
Biology, Astronomy, Math...

Shopping
Auctions, Classifieds, Movies...

Society & Culture
Religion, People, Women...

Sports
Football, Basketball, Baseball...

- FEATURED GUIDES ON LYCOS -

Autos	Health	Real Estate
Business	Home/Family	Reference
Careers	Kids Zone	Sports
Computers	News	Travel
Entertainment	People/Society	Women
Games	Personal Finance	Y2K

More...

Get Lycos in: Belgium, Denmark, France, Germany, Italy, Japan, Korea, Netherlands, Norway,

www.webcrawler.com

"It's that Simple."

- ○ books from **BARNES&NOBLE**
- ○ visit the AT&T Communication Center
- ○ music from CDNOW

Don't Miss: Save $10 on books today!

Search and Channels

[   ] Search

auctions   yellow pages   maps   product finder   books   chat now!
people finder   horoscopes   classifieds   stock quotes   weather
email lookup   city guides   search voyeur   music   more

Arts & Books
best reads, best buys...

Autos
new, used, classifieds...

Careers
write a resume, find a job...

Computers & Internet
software, hardware...

Education
colleges, k-12...

Entertainment
TV, movies, music...

Games
online games, downloads...

Health
diet tips, medical info...

Home & Real Estate
buy, rent, finance...

Kids & Family
CTW family workshop...

Money & Investing
track stocks, invest...

My Page
personalize your page...

News - New!
today's top headlines...

People & Chat - New!
make friends, get advice...

Relationships
advice, personals...

Shopping
deals, product finder...

Small Business
taxes, legal issues...

Sports & Recreation
scores, highlights...

Travel
fares, reservations...

Today on WebCrawler
Find a Cheap Ticket
@Home Cable Internet Access
Free Voicemail Account

Headline News
Updated: Monday, September 20 12:20 PM ET

- o Cuba Jails U.S. Residents For Migrant Smuggling
- o More Than 1,000 UN Troops Arrive In E.Timor
- o Thousands Commemorate Victims Of Texas Shootings

Daily Toolbox

Each day we bring you simple tools to save you time and money.

- o Free Mac & PC Wallpaper
- o How to Treat a Snake Bite
- o Pokemon Finder

See our complete list of tools.

A Word From Our Sponsors...

ibeauty
Great gifts. Free gift wrap. Free shipping.
CDNOW
Top 100 on Sale at CDNOW!
enews.com
Try 650+ magazines - free!

Global Excite: Australia · France · Germany · Japan · Netherlands · Sweden · U.K.
WebCrawler Direct · Bookmark WebCrawler · Advertise on WebCrawler · Add your URL

home || my page || email || help || about Excite

Microsoft Internet Explorer

www.yahoo.com

What's New   Check Email   Personalize   Help

Yahoo! Mail
free email for life   **Instant Stock Alerts**   **Win 1 of
10 Cruises**

[Search] advanced search

Yahoo! Auctions - bid now! Sammy Sosa, photographs, autos, Tony Stewart, Pokemon...

Shopping - **Auctions** - Yellow Pages - People Search - Maps - Travel - Classifieds - Personals - Games - Chat - **Clubs**
Email - Calendar - **Messenger** - My Yahoo! - Today's News - Sports - Weather - TV - Stock Quotes - more...

Arts & Humanities Literature, Photography...	**News & Media** Full Coverage, Newspapers, TV...	**In the News** · Hurricane, storm menace Bermuda, Fla. · Raisa Gorbachev dies · Weekend's top movies · NFL - MLB wild card race more...
Business & Economy Companies, Finance, Jobs...	**Recreation & Sports** Sports, Travel, Autos, Outdoors...	
Computers & Internet Internet, WWW, Software, Games...	**Reference** Libraries, Dictionaries, Quotations...	
Education College and University, K-12...	**Regional** Countries, Regions, US States...	**Marketplace** · Looking for a car? job? house? · Loan Center - auto loans, mortgages, credit reports more...
Entertainment Cool Links, Movies, Humor, Music...	**Science** Animals, Astronomy, Engineering...	
Government Elections, Military, Law, Taxes...	**Social Science** Archaeology, Economics, Languages...	**Inside Yahoo!** · Yahooligans! - for kids · Yahoo! Health - Find a doctor · Y! Greetings - free greeting cards more...
Health Medicine, Diseases, Drugs, Fitness...	**Society & Culture** People, Environment, Religion...	

World Yahoo!s *Europe* : Denmark - France - Germany - Italy - Norway - Spain - Sweden - UK & Ireland
Pacific Rim : Asia - Australia & NZ - Chinese - HK - Japan - Korea - Singapore - Taiwan
Americas : **Brazil** - Canada - Spanish

Yahoo! Get Local LA - NYC - SF Bay - Chicago - more... [Enter Zip Code]

Other Guides Autos - Careers - **Digital** - Entertainment - Health - Local Events - Net Events
Message Boards - Movies - Music - Real Estate - Small Business - Y! Internet Life - Yahooligans!

Yahoo! prefers **VISA**

How to Suggest a Site - Company Info - Privacy Policy - Terms of Service - Contributors - Openings at Yahoo!

Hummel figurines are readily available at www.ebay.com. These four achieved an average selling price of $65.00 each.

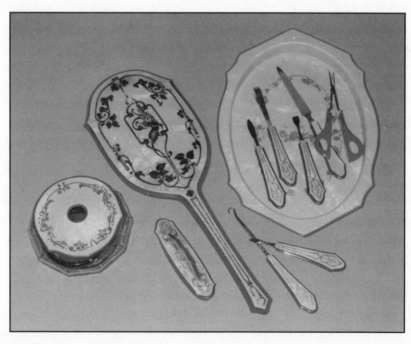

An 11-piece celluloid dresser set purchased at an antique mall for resale on the Internet.

CHAPTER 2
Choose Your Weapon

If you haven't bought a computer yet, you're probably totally confused by the choices. The most basic decision is *PC* (a generic term for personal computer of the IBM or IBM-clone variety) or *Macintosh*, and it gets harder from there. If you already have a computer feel free to skip this chapter unless you're considering upgrading; if not read on and gain useful information that will help you make your decision.

First, I'm not about to get in the middle of the PC versus Macintosh debate—it can get too emotional. People who have used Macs from the beginning swear by them, saying they're more dependable and easier to use. They frequently bristle at the mention of PC users claiming these same traits about their computers. What I will say is this—the vast majority of the business community has turned to the PC. Because of that, most software developers create their programs for the PC, making it much easier to find what you need if you're on a PC platform. The one exception is the graphics arts industry, where the Mac is still viewed as the platform of choice and having a Mac means being more compatible with the rest of the industry. This is also changing, and in fact this book was produced totally on a PC. Unless you intend to use your computer to do desktop publishing in your spare time, choosing a PC will give you many more choices for business applications, schoolwork, and games—the things that many of us like to do when not visiting the online auctions. The introduction of the iMac was aimed specifically at putting a dent in the markets where Macintosh now lags, and while *iMac* has kept Macintosh alive and well it has done little to dethrone the PC as the computer of choice with most users. For now, the PC gives you more choices.

When considering how much power to buy, you need to evaluate how your computer will be used. Processor speeds seem to double from one year to the next so you can be assured that what you buy today will be yesterday's news within six months. What you need to understand about this annoying rule of computer obsolescence is that it doesn't matter how quickly your machine is left behind as long as it does the things you need it to do. In fact, if you're going to use your computer primarily for Internet access and word processing, you definitely don't need the latest and greatest.

A processor with a speed of 233 *megahertz* (Mhz), considered state of the art in 1997, is generally viewed as slow in 1999. Because of being "obsolete," it can be bought for well under $1,000 and will supply all of the raw power you need for basic computing needs. If you plan to work with large image files in a graphic arts environment or play the latest computer games you will want to invest in a faster processor, but for the small files you'll use to post photos on the Internet 233Mhz is plenty.

Your next decision will probably revolve around a choice between a *Pentium* processor versus a *Celeron* processor, both made by *Intel*, or possibly a processor made by competitor *AMD*. Both the Celeron and AMD chipsets got some bad press when they were first introduced, some deservedly so. But if you are purchasing a new computer primarily for Internet access and small office duties, do not hesitate to buy one with either one of these processors. If you want to stick with Intel, the Celeron is a formidable alternative to the more expensive Pentium processors.

To give you an idea of what you can purchase for around $1,000, I recently got a phone call from my daughter who is a graduate student majoring in psychology and has a definite need for some computer power. She was still using an older 120Mhz computer with a 14,400K modem and wanted me to recommend a new system. I offered to do the shopping for her, and came up with the following deal for almost exactly $1,000. Don't worry if you don't understand all of the jargon used here—I'll explain more later.

Dell Dimension 400Mhz Celeron processor with 128K cache
4MB Graphics
Logitech First Mouse+
Dell Quiet Key keyboard
Dell 800F 15" color monitor
32MB SDRAM (we upgraded to 64MB for $59.00 extra)
4.3GB hard drive
1.44MB floppy drive
Soundblaster 64V PCI sound card
Harman/Kardon HK-195 speakers
6X variable DVD-ROM drive
US Robotics V.90 56K telephony WinModem
Epson Stylus 660 color printer
Windows 98
McAfee Virusscan virus software
Microsoft Works Suite99
1 Year DellNet Internet access service

That's right! A 400Mhz computer complete with a color monitor, color printer, 56K modem, a DVD-ROM which also plays CD-ROMs, virus software, office software, a one year warranty and a free year of Internet access for around $1,000! This offering was found on the Internet by buying direct from Dell at http://www.dell.com, proving that good deals are out there.

If you want to hear the sounds (music files, radio, etc.) that the Internet can make, and you will, buy a system with a soundcard and speakers. You should definitely invest in a 56K modem (see Chapter 3— Choosing an Internet Service Provider for more on modems). If you buy a multimedia (MMX) system it should already have the soundcard and speakers bundled right in, but I don't recommend buying MMX technology unless you are purchasing a used machine and are a graphic artist or gaming fanatic. Today's processor speeds make MMX an obsolete technology.

RAM (random access memory) is second in importance to your processor speed when it comes to system performance—the more RAM you get with your computer the better. 32MB is considered standard today, so start there and as you progress you may want to add on. Adding memory is one of the least expensive upgrades you can make, so it won't be costly if you decide you want more later.

The *SDRAM* mentioned in the computer my daughter purchased is *synchronous dynamic random access memory*, which is faster than previous generations of random access memory. It sends data from the main memory to the system processor more efficiently, and is a must for computers that utilize the new 100Mhz bus speeds. You should make sure you are getting SDRAM with any new computer purchase.

Your *hard drive* is where everything you need to operate your computer is stored. Hard drives are rated in terms of the amount of data they can hold. Just a few years ago the largest hard drives were rated in megabytes (MB), but today are measured in gigabytes (GB). To help you comprehend the amount of data we're talking about here, know that a single character is the equivalent of one *byte*. From there measurements are as follows...

1024 Bytes = 1 Kilobyte
1024 Kilobytes = 1 Megabyte
1024 Megabytes = 1 Gigabyte
1024 Gigabytes = 1 Terabyte

Most software today is loaded onto your computer from a *CD-ROM*. The faster the drive the more quickly large applications should be loaded. However, some software manufacturers prepare their data in a format that only allows your CD-ROM to read them at slower speeds, so having the fastest drive isn't critical.

Games are played from CD-ROMs, and the same music CDs you listen to in your car or home CD player will play in your computer CD-ROM drive (provided of course you have the proper software, a soundcard, and speakers). A 32X drive has become fairly common, but don't fret if the computer you like best has a slower drive. Unless you are a gaming fanatic you probably won't notice much difference.

The next evolution of the CD-ROM is already here in the form of the *DVD-ROM*. DVD-ROM brings enhanced multimedia capabilities to your system, including the ability to watch movies on it. DVD-ROM is backward compatible with CD-ROM, so your software installation CD's will still work and you can still play your audio CDs. At the present time movies on DVD-ROM are just beginning to surface, but they will be as prolific as VHS in the future.

Unless you buy a package like the one outlined earlier in this chapter you will have to purchase a monitor separately from your computer. Special offers will sometimes bundle them together, but more often than not when you purchase a computer you don't get the monitor with it. A 14-inch monitor may have you squinting occasionally and a 17-inch monitor is an unnecessary expense unless you routinely work with page layout spreads or spreadsheets. A 15-inch monitor is fine for general use, but as prices come down a 17-inch monitor, once considered a luxury, will become much more common on home systems.

Be aware that the resolution of the monitor affects the size and clarity of your display. Though I'm not sure where you might find one, anything less than a resolution of 640x480 is unacceptable today. You can change the resolution of your monitor through the Control Panel of your computer. On a Windows 95 or 98 computer click **Start-Settings-Control Panel**. In the window that opens double-click **Display**. The resulting window will have a tab you can click for **Settings**. You will now see a slide bar that controls the resolution of your monitor and can experiment with different settings until you get the one you're most comfortable with.

Also check the *refresh rate* of the video card driving the monitor. The refresh rate is the speed with which it redraws an image on the screen.

Video cards are rated in *Hz* (hertz), which is the amount of electrical pulses emitted per second. Don't settle for anything less than a 60Hz refresh rate.

The 1.44MB floppy disk has been a standard for years, and unless you come across a real relic at a yard sale every PC you find will have one. The name "floppy" was derived from the earliest days of computing, when the first home computers used a removable disk measuring 5.25" in diameter that really was flexible, and would "flop" around when you held it by one corner. Macintosh computers also make use of a floppy, although unless you have special "decoding" software a PC cannot read a Mac disk and vice versa.

Macintosh gambled with the introduction of their iMac and did not equip them with floppy disk drives, reasoning that the floppy was obsolete and that the future was the Internet and larger storage capacity. I believe this to be sound reasoning, but Macintosh may have been a bit ahead of their time. The average computer user still needs a floppy drive, and until the benefits of the larger capacity removable storage drives are recognized by the overall business community, floppies still reign supreme.

If you are in the graphic arts business and routinely move large graphic files from place to place, you should definitely opt for a built-in Iomega ZIP or JAZ drive. The ZIP comes in either a 100MB or 250MB size, utilizing a removable cartridge that is not much bigger than a floppy. The JAZ cartridge is a bit bigger yet, but can hold either 1GB or 2GB of data.

Here then is my recommendation for a basic PC that you intend to use primarily for word processing, Internet access, and general use. This is actually a generously powered machine, but in today's market there's not enough difference in price to buy any less. Talk to the vendor you purchase your computer from about your needs and ask them to recommend and explain additional features available. You can purchase a computer with these specifications for less than $1000, and if you look hard enough you will be able to include the monitor and a printer for that price.

233Mhz Processor
32MB RAM
3.2GB Hard Drive
1.44MB Floppy Drive
32X CD ROM Drive
15-Inch Color Monitor (640x480 resolution minimum)
4MB video card w/60Hz Refresh Rate
56K Modem
Soundcard
Speakers

If you already have a computer with Internet access and are considering upgrading, you might want to get your feet wet with online auctions by bidding on computers and/or computer parts. Most of the major online auctions have a computer category, and mail order companies like PC Mall hold online auctions at their sites too.

Two Roseville vases found on eBay.

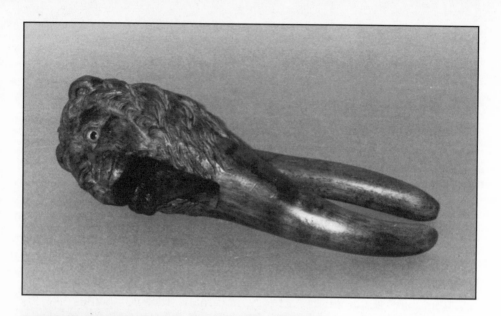

A wooden nutcracker with a lion's head. Animal collectibles are easy to find on Internet Auctions.

A Capo-di-monte type pitcher with a lion handle and relief figures.

CHAPTER 3
Choosing an Internet Service Provider

You have a computer with a modem, now what? How do you find an Internet Service Provider (*ISP*)? How do you sift through the seemingly endless technology offerings of the different providers? You don't have to understand the difference between a SLIP/PPP and UUCP connection, but you should be able to recognize a good deal from an average one.

Finding an Internet Service Provider
Start by asking your friends and business associates who they use. They should be able to provide phone numbers for you to begin your quest and possibly even promotional disks from an ISP with some free hours to try their service. The national ISPs, particularly *America Online* and *Earthlink*, distribute a large number of these trial disks.

The newspapers, especially in larger metropolitan areas, will likely have ads for local providers you can contact. As you read on you will find information to help you evaluate whether you want to try a national or local provider.

Don't overlook the major phone companies—AT&T, Sprint, MCI, Bell Atlantic, and many others all provide Internet access. If you're in the market for a local provider try the phone book under categories like Computers-Communications or Internet Service Providers.

Here are some questions to ask an Internet Service Provider you are considering.

√ Do you have a local access number?
Avoid dialing long distance to connect to your ISP, unless you live in a remote area and have no choice. When your ISP is a long distance call away, you pay not only their monthly access charge but also long distance charges to your phone company for the ENTIRE time you are connected. The national carriers provide local numbers for large metropolitan areas, but there are still regions where they are not available. If this happens to you, investigate whether or not you have a regional/local company offering Internet access. If you do, consider signing up with them as long as they satisfy the requirements outlined in this chapter.

If one of the national providers offers things you really want (some people can't live without their America Online chat rooms) you might be able to make a special arrangement with a local ISP to use their service as a way to get connected to the national provider. You'll be paying a monthly fee to both, but it still might be lower than paying long distance charges for access. Make sure you let the national provider know you are paying double to get their service because they have no local access number and ask for a reduced rate.

√ Do you use SLIP/PPP?

Here's one of those technical terms we're trying to avoid, but this is one you should ask. With SLIP/PPP, you have direct access to the Internet through your ISPs server. Some ISPs route you through a series of computers and servers before you actually connect. There are many reasons why you should connect directly, the most obvious being speed and less chance of downtime. The more computers you pass through on your way to the Internet the better chance you have of one of them breaking your connection. Suffice to say you want the direct access provided by SLIP/PPP—don't settle for less. And for those of you who just have to know, SLIP is an acronym for Serial Line Internet Protocol and PPP is Point-to-Point Protocol. There, feel better?

√ What types of accounts do you offer?

Most ISPs will offer at least a monthly rate for unlimited service and an hourly, or metered rate. Some offer discounts to senior citizens and students—be sure to ask.

√ What is your ratio of subscribers to modems?

The more modems your ISP has the better. A good ratio if you have unlimited access is 9:1 (nine users to one modem) and for metered access 14:1. Higher numbers don't necessarily spell trouble, but unusually high ratios can mean busy signals when you dial in and slower connection speeds.

√ What is the cost for each type of account?

Monthly charges vary more than you might think. I've seen monthly rates for unlimited access as low as $9.95 for a local ISP in a rural area to $26.95 for the bigger national providers. Make sure you inquire about installation fees—some charge them even though the "installation" is done from their office. In the beginning you might consider opting for the higher cost provider if they offer top-notch tech support to help you through the learning curve. Once you're a savvy user consider switching to the low-cost provider if they meet your basic requirements.

√ Do you charge for disk space on your server?

When you start taking photos with that new digital camera you couldn't live without you'll need space on your ISP's server to post them for the world to see. If you're in the market for an unlimited access account look for a provider that offers some server space as a part of your monthly fee. Many offer 2 megabytes at no additional charge, and this is adequate for the average user.

√ Will my modem talk to your modem?

Modems are like "walkie-talkies" for computers. If your computer has one, and it is connected to a phone line, you can "talk" to someone else who has another modem. Unlike walkie-talkies, modems simply transfer information bits; you don't actually speak. But modems are the lifeblood of sending and receiving information on the Internet and using e-mail.

Modems come in both external (sits on your desk) and *internal* (resides inside your computer) varieties, and computer people used to argue endlessly about which was best. They're priced about the same, and the fact is they both perform about the same, so it comes down to whether or not you like to watch flashing lights when you're sending data. I recommend going with an internal modem, even though it may cost a few dollars more to have a professional install it in your computer. The less clutter on your desk the better!

Most modems will connect to each other, but with newer technologies being invented all the time you should ask the question. Hopefully you know your modem speed and manufacturer—if not, check the *Control Panel* of a computer running Windows. You will see a modem icon: double click it and you will get some general information about your modem, which may help the ISP you are talking to determine if you are compatible with their system. If you don't know what type of modem you have and can't find out, ask if there is a test you can perform that will assure you can connect with them. At the very worst you may have to buy a new, higher speed modem, which isn't a bad idea anyway if you're using one several years old. Less than $100 will get you a top-notch model, but you may go a bit over $100 if someone else installs it for you.

Modem speeds are measured in kilo-bits per second (Kbps) along with a number rating. If you have a modem with a top speed of 14,400 or 28,800 consider upgrading to at least 33,600 and preferably 56,000 (56K in computer lingo). These higher speed modems have dropped considerably in price since first being introduced. If you opt for a 56K modem be sure you get one that uses the recently adopted V.90 standard; all ISPs are required to support modems with this technology.

√ How many mail accounts do I get?

This may be explained to you when you ask about the types of accounts, but if it isn't make sure you're getting at least one e-mail address. Without one, you can't send or receive electronic mail unless you subscribe to one of the free Internet-hosted services. These accounts, offered on the home page of several major search engines, are often slow and cumbersome to use. You will quickly find that your own ISP-provided e-mail account is one of the most useful reasons for having Internet access.

√ Do you offer all available newsgroups?

Newsgroups are informative and entertaining, and as you become more experienced you'll find yourself subscribing to a few. You can interact with an international audience about almost anything you can imagine, including your favorite collectibles.

Individual newsgroups are formed to discuss one primary topic. The term *Usenet* refers to the entire newsgroup community collectively. Newsgroup names begin with a prefix that denotes a general guide to their category. These categories are expanding constantly, but some of the types of groups you will encounter are...

alt	Discussion of alternative/informal subjects
comp	Discussion of computer science and related topics
news	Discussion of Usenet itself
rec	Discussion of recreational activities
sci	Discussion of scientific research
talk	Debate on controversial issues
misc	Groups that don't fall into established categories

Specific newsgroups exist for dolls (**rec.collecting.dolls**), teddy bears (**alt.collecting.teddy-bears**), and many other collectibles. Some newsgroups contain primarily items for sale, but some share information, and the things you can learn by participating in one or two good ones about your favorite collectible is amazing. Some of the groups are very active, with hundreds of messages being posted daily. Others have less traffic; feel free to monitor several until you find one that seems comfortable. You should be able to access newsgroups from your e-mail program, as well as search for newsgroups containing a certain word or words you specify (i.e. antiques).

Be aware that certain newsgroups have controversial subjects as their content, and some ISPs censor these. If you're planning to join a newsgroup with content you think may be at risk, inquire as to whether all newsgroups are supported.

Once you've signed on, always remember when communicating with groups to choose your words carefully—more than one novice newsgroup user has been *flamed* by the group for a poor choice of vocabulary or topic. Flaming is the online equivalent of the lecture you got from your mother when you were bad, but is often a lot nastier than good old Mom would have been. Seeing it in print can have a more negative impact than the spoken word, and the fact that you're being flamed by virtual strangers makes it very uncomfortable. It's a good idea to just read the posts from a newsgroup that interests you for a week or two before jumping in. This way you can get a feel for the types of people you'll be interacting with.

√ How does your tech support work?

Is it staffed 24 hours? If not, what hours may I call and what is the number? If the call is not local, do you have a toll free number? Do you have a Web site and/or online support? Will you help me configure my computer to communicate with your equipment? Is there any software I have to buy in order to communicate with your equipment?

Once you have the answers to all of these questions, call the tech support number to see if you get a live person, a recording, or get put on indefinite hold. Anything other than a live person answering relatively quickly should go in the minus column when considering this ISP.

Once you choose your ISP you have one more decision to make—whether or not you want to invest in a second phone line for your Internet access. If you plan to do a lot of online business it's pretty much a necessity. Even a part-time business online takes more time than you are probably thinking. As outlined in my companion book to this one, **The ABCs of Making Money Online**, the biggest surprise for most dealers expanding their business to the Internet is the time investment it takes. That time online takes away from time your spouse and kids can spend talking on the phone, so consider a second line if for no other reason than to keep peace in the family.

Another thing you will want to consider is your phone bills and how to minimize costs. As stated earlier in this chapter, your first priority is to make sure the number you dial to connect is a local number. Next, find out if you are paying a flat rate for unlimited local calls. If you're not, you might want to switch to a flat rate depending on how often you plan to dial in to your ISP. If unlimited local calling is not available, inquire about *call packs*, which allow you to call the same phone number a specified amount of times for a flat fee.

You are now armed and ready to begin an adventure in learning the likes of which you've never seen. Be warned: the Internet is addictive!

A brass 7-candle sconce purchased at auction for resale on the Internet.

A circa 1885 Eastlake style armchair. Furniture is widely available online.

This footstool with Queen Anne style legs was purchased for $55.00 at www.ebay.com.

CHAPTER 4
Finding Antiques and Collectibles in Cyberspace

There are many choices available online for buying and selling antiques and collectibles. The one used by more people than any other is eBay™, an online auction that routinely offers close to three million items in so many different categories you can't possibly look at everything in the week it takes for a typical auction to expire. If you haven t already, read Chapter 5 - Using eBay™ to get the details. Once you know your way around eBay™ you can feel secure in trying out some other online auctions. Most of them operate in similar ways, and as you become familiar with buying this way you will find it easy to navigate through any online auction site.

Literally thousands of sites exist on the Internet to buy or sell antiques and collectibles. Some are general and sell a wide variety of merchandise, while others are specific to a certain type, say jewelry. Some are auctions and some are online malls or individual shops. You can use search engines to find and explore this array of possibilities, but to help get you started, following is a list of some of the ones I've visited. Many of these were launched during 1998 with some being even newer. None of them have yet achieved anywhere near the visibility or volume of listings as eBay™.

What will you find online in the antiques and collectibles fields? It would be easier to list the things you won't find. Furniture, not as widely available at the online auctions at one time due mainly to the costs associated with shipping, has become commonplace. Buyers are paying as much as $250 to have large pieces shipped to them after winning auctions. Many online malls and individual shops also offer furniture, including some very high quality pieces.

The top ten sought after collectibles online varies weekly. During the late summer of 1998 Mark McGwire and Sammy Sosa collectibles were in high demand as they both chased, and eventually broke, the major league baseball home run record set by Roger Maris in 1961. *BARBIE*® and Morgan silver dollars often make the top ten, probably due to the fact that they are well-known and therefore popular with new collectors, and so many were produced. But no matter what collectible interests you, there is a very good chance you will be able to find it at an online auction.

General Auctions

The information about the following online auctions was researched during September and October 1999. In reviewing these auctions, it seemed that the different sites, whether by choice or not, were "specializing" in certain items. One site might have primarily Beanie Babies for sale, while another might have predominantly sports cards. Whether this trend will continue remains to be seen, but for now it seems collectors congregate at the auction site which becomes "known" for the particular items they seek. Nearly all of the smaller sites that were predominantly one type of collectible last year when the first edition of this book was being written are still "specializing" in that same collectible this year.

http://auctions.amazon.com

The "World's Biggest Bookstore" has entered the online auction world. Amazon.com offers a buyer's guarantee that says you will receive your item and it will be as described by the seller or they will refund your purchase price up to a $250 limit.

http://www.auctionaddict.com

Auction Addict has an attractive site that features no listing fees. As one of the many newcomers to the online auction world during 1998, listings at first were few when compared to some of the established auctions. However, Auction Addict has grown and whereas their largest category in late 1998 was Collectibles with 324 listings, that category in September 1999 was still largest but boasted over 2200 entries. Overall, there were 21 categories with almost 9000 open listings.

Auction Addict has also redesigned their site since the first edition of this book, eliminating the use of *frames*. Web pages using frames means having two or more windows display at the same time. Some web authors stay away from frames at all cost, as older browsers have problems interpreting them and some people feel it adds too much "clutter" to a page. Auction Addict now has a cleaner, simpler, and easier to navigate site.

http://www.auctionport.com

Auction Port continues to survive in the online auction world, with 1759 entries in a wide range of categories, roughly a 40% increase in volume from a year ago. The site is well designed, easy to use, and features chat forums with some of the categories. There are no basic listing fees to sellers.

http://www.auctions.com

This site was formerly Auction Universe, with the new name and a completely redesigned site being launched October 12, 1999. The redesigned site is easy to use, loads more quickly, has a good variety to choose from, and offers free basic listings. A recent check showed 30,164 total items up for bid, a 30% increase from the 21,413 items found eight months ago during research for the first edition of this book. Once again the Sports Collectibles category was the most prolific at this site, numbering 16,339 or a whopping 54% of the total listings. Beanie Babies were next, with 4255 listings. It is interesting to note that just these two categories make up over two-thirds of the listings on the entire site.

http://www.auctionworks.com

Calling themselves "Antiques, Computers, Collectibles and more..." you might be surprised to find that Auction Works has no category dedicated to antiques. There are a few antiques scattered through the collectible categories, but nothing dedicated to just antiques. Actually there was not much to choose from at all, with only 99 active listings in mid-September 1999. As was the case a year ago, in most categories all active listings were by the same seller, giving the impression that not too many people visit this site.

http://www.buffalobid.com

Buffalo Bid continues to be a thriving auction site, particularly in the postcard and coin categories. There were 2053 active listings when I checked, more than double the 975 listings nearly a year ago. Coins/Currency and Postcards were the leading categories last year too, fortifying my contention that the smaller sites attract specific followings, and once a trend is established it continues. There aren't many antiques here, but there are just enough collectibles to make it interesting. Photos are viewed separately from the listings, which is somewhat inconvenient and downright annoying on a day when busy Internet traffic makes browsing slow.

http://www.buyit.com

The BuyIt Web site, like most others established during the past year, has already had a face lift to improve looks. Now if only BuyIt had improved their performance! The good news—there are many more listings in September 1999 than there were in late 1998. The bad news—when you click on the Listings link to see them, be prepared to wait a long, long time for the page to load. Every listing is on the same page, and the category links that would eliminate having to wade through hundreds of irrelevant listings are at the bottom of this page, so you don't get to them until it's too late. Bad design and too much wait time make this site too bulky for impatient Web surfers to use.

http://www.ebay.com

After almost four years eBay™ is still the king of the hill, having withstood the charge (so far) of Amazon.com and Yahoo! auctions. Instead of losing business to these challengers, eBay™ has increased in volume, routinely offering over 2.5 million items for sale at the same time. Less than a year ago, that number was 700,000. A recent site redesign gave eBay™ a more modern look, and their huge volume means that it s unusual to not find what you're looking for. See Chapter 5 - Using eBay™ for step-by-step instructions on how to register and get going.

http://www.coymedia.com/auctions

A large site with a bit of everything including hardware, sporting goods, tickets and travel as well as antiques and collectibles. Coy is the self-proclaimed second largest independent online marketplace and auction site in the world.

http://www.cyrbid.com

Cyr auction, based in Maine, has started an online auction that is definitely one to watch. During their launch month of September 1999 there were many high quality antiques and collectibles sold with no reserve and going for very fair prices. As traffic increases, so might prices, but the fact that they are listing items found in old New Hampshire country stores should be enough to tell you it's worth looking at.

http://www.ehammer.com

This site was launched with a lot of advertising and, being backed by *Maine Antique Digest*, I expected it by this time to be a leader in the online auction community. In some ways it is—the ratio of high quality items to overall listings is unmatched in the online auction world. Total listings numbered just 2,746 in late September 1999, but as mentioned, the quality of the antiques is first rate. e-Hammer also claims an average selling price of three times more than the average selling price recorded on other sites, which may well be true due to the high-end merchandise listed there.

http://www.gomainline.com

A growing site dedicated to just antiques and collectibles. Go Main Line is focusing on quality merchandise and value added services like experts you can contact with your questions about antiques and collectibles.

http://www.haggle.com

Primarily computers and electronics—if you deal in these items this is one to check out.

http://www.skybid.com

Another well-advertised new launch, SkyBid had 276 registered users and 284 listings two weeks after beginning operations. A month later, registered users had increased to 904, although total listings had increased only to 309. Now, nearly a year later, SkyBid has garnered only 2695 registered users and had only 18 items listed when I checked in. At this point in time, SkyBid appears to be an also-ran bordering on obscurity.

http://www.up4sale.com

"Free Auctions Forever" is the Up4Sale motto, and it seems to be drawing an audience. Antiques & Collectibles, Computers & Equipment, and General Merchandise are the three main categories offered, with each having many subcategories. Beanie Babies were abundant, with over 19,000 available. Trading cards were also well represented with over 5,000 being offered. Though I found few genuine antiques, this is a site well worth checking out for collectibles.

http://auctions.yahoo.com

Yahoo! is free to registered users for both buying and selling, and offers you different choices on ending your auctions. You can have the auction automatically extended until the bidding stops for a specified time to discourage sniping if you wish.

http://auctions.amazon.com

amazon.com
🛒 | YOUR ACCOUNT | HELP

WELCOME | BOOKS | MUSIC | VIDEO | TOYS & GAMES | ELECTRONICS | e-CARDS | AUCTIONS

ADVANCED SEARCH | BROWSE CATEGORIES | AUCTIONS HELP | YOUR AUCTIONS | SELL YOUR ITEM NOW

SEARCH AUCTIONS

[   ] GO!

BROWSE

- **Art & Antiques**
- **Books**
- **Ceramics & Glass**
- **Clothing & Accessories**
- **Coins & Stamps**
- **Collectibles**
- **Comics, Cards & Sci-Fi**
- **Computers & Software**
- **Electronics & Photography**
- **Gemstones & Jewelry**
- **Home & Garden**
- **Movies & Video**
- **Music**
- **Office & Business**
- **Other Goods & Services**
- **Sports & Recreation**
- **Toys & Games**
  ▶ See all categories...

WELCOME TO Amazon.com Auctions

Items Featured Today

- 11 PIECE INDOOR/OUTDOOR GARDENING TOOL KITS WITH CA
- Genuine Leather Jacket BLOWOUT!!! Only $35 !! CHECK IT OUT!!!!!
- LOSE~ALL~THE~WEIGHT~YOU~WANT~OR~YOUR~MONEY~BA
- *** SAPPHIRE BRACELET *** CLEARANCE - HOT!!!
- X-FILES "I Want to Believe" FULL-COLOR POSTER
- The Best Michael Jordan Upper Deck Authenticated Signed Nike Sneak

⬤ Apply to sell on Sothebys.amazon.com

⬤ Bid at Live Auctions with **Live Bid**

What's Happening

- Get a chance to own a few of Oprah Winfrey's priceless possessions! Network Auction on October 2.
- Learn about Halper's legendary baseball collection and order your co volume auction preview catalog today.
  ▶ See all happenings...

Last Updated: September 20, 1999 10:46:30 PST

Text Only   Top of Page
Amazon.com Home | Books | Music | Video | Toys & Games | Electronics | e-Cards | Auctions | 1-Click Settings
| Shopping Cart | Your Account | Help

Auction Search | Browse Categories | Getting Started | Your Auctions | Sell an Item Now

Amazon.co.uk | Amazon.de

AuctionAddict.com

Search the Auction and Classified Ads for [   ] [go]

Monday, 20-Sep-99 12:41:44 EDT

Getting Started   Search   Sell   Customer Service   Account Master

Antiques (62)
Automotive (55)
Books & Magazines (541)
Coins & Currency (62)
Collectibles (2259)
Computers (1183)
Consumer Electronics (311)
Food & Wine (32)
Home Furnishings (474)
Jewelry & Gems (584)
Laboratory & Medical (28)
Memorabilia (338)
Miscellaneous (667)
Movies & Music (388)
Musical Instruments (65)
Services & Information (115)
Sporting Goods (165)
Stamps (343)
Toys (598)
Trading Cards (591)
Travel (27)

View all the categories...

What is this Place?

Register Now, It's Free!

List an Item

Featured Today...

- BEAUTIFUL HAND CRAFTED CHILDREN'S DESK $45.00
- "Arts and Crafts" Solid Wood Mission Dining Set $2450.00
- WEB HOSTING STARTING AT $10.95/M, EXTRA FREE STUFF $0.01
- Micron Laptop without Micron's Price! $250.00
- "SONY NOTEBOOK FOR LESS! .9 INCH PROFILE, LIGHTWEIGHT 3.5 $550.0
- DELL NOTEBOOK WITHOUT DELL'S PRICE!!!! $1250.00
- "AMD K62 3D 400 /17"/ 44x/ 64mb/8G/AGP/3D/56k" $350.00
- "Intell PIII 550 w/ 21"M BEST OF EVERYTHING !" $2598.00
- "Intel PIII 500 + 19"+DVD/256M/27G/ATI32/SB/+" $900.00
- "Intel PIII 450 17"/DVD/128M/13G/ATI32/56k/SB+" $800.00
- $9, Dual LNB RCA DSS system, Complete, No Reserve $15.00
- Take Your Pet Anywhere You Go! $15.00

Did you also know...

- This is a great place to sell your large, big ticket items. All our listings are categorized and searchable by geographic region, so that you can view things like cars located near you.

- Your business can have its own full featured auction or e-commerce website using our award-winning technology. Forget about IT and customer service headaches... Outsource your e-commerce needs to the experts. AuctionAddict.com will design, host, and maintain your site for you, and have it ready for launch in under 30 days. Find out more...

Quick Searches

- Items ending within 10 minutes...
- Items ending within 3 hours...
- Items under $2
- Items under $5
- Items under $10

http://www.auctionaddict.com/

http://www.auctionport.com

AuctionPort
The Best Antiques, Collectibles and More That Auctions Have To Offer

Home   Listings   Register   Buyers   Sellers   Live   Rooms   Featured   Ending   Search   Help   Guide

Monday, September 20, 1999 13:27:58 ET

[Search] options

Check out what's new at Auction Port!

Antiques & Art
Big Ticket Items
Books & Magazines
Coins & Currency
Collectibles
Computers
Consumer
Dolls & Figures
Glass
Jewelry & Timepieces
Miscellaneous
Music & Movies
Pottery & Porcelain
Sports & Trading Cards
Stamps
Toys
all categories...

Personal Online Auctions and the **Auction Port Gallery**
"An Antique and Collectibles Experience"

Welcome to Auction Port Online Auctions, click for how to get started with our easy and fun auction community. Auction Port has no basic insertion or listing fee and it's always free to the buyer. Auction Port Online Auction registration is not required to browse the community >>>...any questions?

Highlights	**User Resources**	**Auction Rooms**
Auctions Ending	**Personal Shopper**	**Auction Port Gallery**
New Auctions	**Appraisal Wizard**	**Annabelle's Angel's**
Hot Auctions	**Live Chat Forums**	**Sophias Collectibles**
Hot Categories	**Free Classifieds**	*....auction room sign up*
Live Auctions	**Wish List Board**	
Auctions Just Listed	**Bookstore**	
.....more auction features	**Internet Resources**	
	.....more resources	

See These Featured Auctions....

📷 = See Photo Now   Description = Go to Item   ® = Reserve Auction

NEW! 📷	**RARE BENRUS COMPLICATED 10KT 17 JEWEL MENS WATCH**	Seen: 0	Current: **$59.99**	Ends: 10/4 10:12 AM ET
NEW! 📷 ®	**36x25 oil painting by Werner Kontor**	Seen: 10	Current: **$1000.00**	Ends: 10/19 9:24 AM ET
	Habanos Cohiba Robusto box 25 Sealed,Cuban!!	Seen: 4	Current: **$335.00**	Ends: 9/28 9:23 PM ET
	Island Habanos Partagas 8-9-8 sealed box 25	Seen: 2	Current: **$330.00**	Ends: 9/28 9:17 PM ET
	Habanos Romeo Y Julieta petits coronas sealed box	Seen: 1	Current: **$335.00**	Ends: 9/28 9:11 PM ET
	EASY,HEALTHY,LOWFAT COOKBOOK BLOWOUT SALE!! WOW!	Seen: 1	Current: **$8.25**	Ends: 10/18 7:04 PM ET
📷	Vintage Knight with Shield and Sword	Seen: 2	Current: **$5.00**	Ends: 10/2 2:20 PM ET
📷	Making Magic Plate by Robert Anderson Little Girls	Seen: 0	Current: **$8.00**	Ends: 10/2 2:20 PM ET

>>> **see more featured....**

apartments.com
Take a Virtual Tour...

Alabama ▼ | GO!

  SEARCH

Advanced Search ▷ View All Categories ▷ My auctions.com ▷ Merchant Central ▷ Showcase Auctions! ▷

Getting Started: How to Sell and Bid | Register Free | List an Item | Shop | Site Help | Contact Us

Categories

▷ **Antiques & Decorative Arts**
▷ **Autos, Boats, Planes**
▷ **Beanies and More Beans**
▷ **Books, Autographs & Paper**
▷ **Business Goods & Services**
▷ **Comics, Cards, Figures, SciFi**
▷ **Computers**
▷ **Dolls, Toys & Models**
▷ **Electronics**
▷ **Home, Garden & Pet Supplies**
▷ **Jewelry & Fashion**
▷ **Music, TV & Entertainment**
▷ **Other Collectibles**
▷ **Other Memorabilia**
▷ **Real Estate & Properties**
▷ **Sporting Goods & Recreation**
▷ **Sports Cards & Collectibles**
▷ **Stamps, Coins & Currency**
▷ **Grab Bag**
see all categories >>

our partner sites:

Auctions in Australia
Auctions in the United Kingdom
apartments.com
cars.com
HomeHunter sites
MovingCenter
NewHomeNetwork.com

Feature Charity Event

"The Chicago Cows on Parade" exhibit is MOOving out of the city and into the country. Bid on Bovines November 1st thru November 9th. **Preview the cows and register now at** metromix.com

auctions.com is e-powering the online cow auction. Check it out!

COWntdown
12 days
Until Auction

Featured Item

Asian art at its best! You won't find quality like this just anywhere. This Japanese Takara would make a great addition to any collection. Click here to bid!

Welcome to auctions.com!

New features. New benefits. New possibilities.

Merchants

ValueVision
Beautiful gems and jewels at unbeatable savings!

▷ **Furniture Find Auctions**
We bet you'll never find better deals!

▷ **Merchants Online**
Shop with our top merchants. Bargains abound!

▷ **Merchant Central**
Your own auction page or site!

▷ **Tops4Less**
Accessorize your car or truck at unbeatable savings!

TRUST·e
site privacy statement

An Online Commerce and Auction Experience

How to Sell and Bid | Register Free | List an Item | Shop | Site Help | Contact Us

http://www.auctionworks.com

Auctions

- List by category
- Search the auctions
- Featured Auctions
- New Auctions
- Starting Today
- Ending Today
- List all auctions
- Live Auction List
- Live Auction Rooms

Search For Lot #:

[_____] Submit

Services

- Seller Services
- Buyer Services
- E-Check Payment System !
- Register - It's FREE!
- Confirm Registration
- Unconfirmed Registrations
- Personal Shopper
- Automated Response
- Discussion Group
- Wish List
- Chat Room
- Secure Exchange

Information

AUCTIONWORKS
Antiques, Computers, Collectibles and more...

[×|_____]

Welcome **News** **Surveys** **Features**

NO LISTING FEES!*

In order to welcome you to our auction service, we've waived the listing fees! If your item doesn't sell, you pay nothing! Look over the Services and fees page for more information on placing items on the auction. *(Featured Item and Bold listing fee's excluded)*

Not sure how to use the service?

Want to sell or buy an item on the auction, but you aren't sure how to do it? Then check out our How-to page and FAQ page. Everything you need to get started! Also see our Technical Support page for problem solutions!

Discussion Group & Chat Room

We've opened the Discussion Group and Chat Room for our registered users! Be sure to drop in and join the other registered user in some fun!

Featured Auctions

#19507: 'LONDON BRIDGE' Commemorative Opening Edition

Antiques - Collectibles - Postcards - Coins - Stamps - Western Memorabilia - Paper & Ephemera & More!

Welcome to

Buffalo Bid Antique Auction

Antiques, Collectibles, Western Memorabilia & Other Good Stuff!

Never a Fee To Buyers!

FREE Regular Listings & FREE Picture Uploads!

Register Now - Free!

View Listings	Open an Account	Sell an Item
Seller Services	Buyer Services	User Services
New	Ending	Search
Featured	Rules	Fees

Contact Us (the Buffalo Loves Mail)
Have you registered at Buffalobid and not received confirmation?
You can check our unconfirmed registration list!

Join the Buffalo's mailing list!
Enter your email address below,
then click the 'Join List' button:

Powered by ListBot

Bookmark This Page Now!

http://www.buyit.com

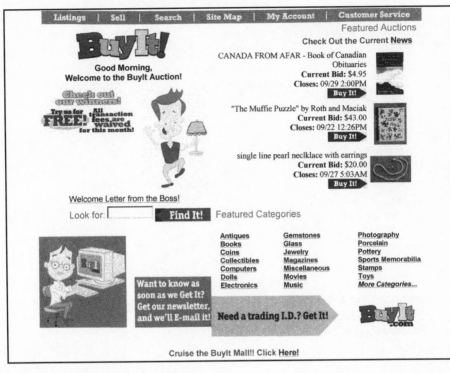

Cruise the BuyIt Mall!! Click Here!

http://www.ebay.com

http://www.coymedia.com/auctions

categories

(301) antiques
(532) arts & crafts
(23) aviation
(837) books/music/movies
(163) clothing
(130) coins/currency/stamps
(1742) collectibles
(1242) computers
(226) dolls/figures
(357) electronics
(62) entertainment
(128) equipment & supplies
(90) food & beverage
(163) furniture
(94) glassware
(104) hardware & appliances
(178) health & beauty
(451) jewelry & gems
(389) memorabilia
(22) metalware
(531) miscellaneous
(97) music & instruments
(53) photography
(46) religious
(81) services
(182) sporting goods
(106) sports
(103) tickets & travel
(87) tools & parts
(240) toys
(859) trading cards
(228) transportation
(279) video games

**Coy Media
Auction House**

welcome to Coy Media Online Auction House in association with **utrade.com**

it's all FREE
That's right. Pay nothing to list or sell your stuff. It's all free, everywhere, anytime.

selling online
Want extra cash? Then, sell your stuff. If you're new, it's easy to do.

finding stuff
Browse the listings
Search the auctions
SiteMap

bidding & buying
If you're new, you'll want to start here.

other stuff
questions or comments?
write to us at support@utrade.com

> **Shortcuts** ▼

helpful links

shop around

what are you looking for? search here.

[ ] **GO**

super deals
Auctions closing in one hour
Auctions closing today

seller services

you've never sold here
Selling basics
Seller frequently asked questions
Put something up for sale
you've sold items here
Feedback
Add an Item(s)
Transaction Management

top storefronts
Collectible Treasures
Stallings Stained Glass
Gehron's Gallery
The Recycle Bin
House of History
As Seen On TV
more storefronts...

buyer services

you've never bought here
Become a buyer
How to bid on something
you have bought here
Advanced search
myUtrade

http://www.cyrbid.com

cyrbid
Your Online Auction for Antiques and Collectibles

search [_____] Go
Advanced | Tips

Browse Antiques | Browse Collectibles

Getting Started

Antiques

Collectibles

Bulletin Boards

Why Cyr?

Sign up Now! IT'S FREE!

Featured Spotlight Item

Title: Early Crank Sewing Machine

Description: Early claw foot iron crank sewing machine with Painted Decoration

Current Bid: $101.00

# of bids: 16

Time Left: 5 Days 21h 7m

Welcome to the debut of cyrbid! **Sign Up** now - it's easy and free!

Themes & Events

THIS WEEK:
- **Potpourri** (anything goes!)

UPCOMING THEMES:

9/27 - **Arts & Crafts Week**

10/4 - **Photography Week**

10/11 - **Toys Week**

10/18 - **Americana Week**

view the Theme Calendar...

Featured Auctions

Auction Title	Current Bid
Signed Tiffany Favrille Bowl	$150.00
Pair Signed Sevres Cache Pot	$800.00
Miniature Painting On Ivory	$102.00
Wonderful Pair Triple Overlay Boheman Vases	$800.00
Fine Painting On Tile	$90.00
Gilt & Decorated Haviland Pitcher	$38.50
Decorated Nippon Ewer	$123.02
Early Crank Sewing Machine	$101.00
Fine Satsuma Cup and Saucer	$16.00
Great Marble & Bronze Mantle Clock	$550.00
Quezal Lamp Shades	$350.00

more..

more Featured Auctions...

cyrbid Magazine

FEATURING THIS WEEK:

WELCOME TO CYRBID - Read about what makes cyrbid different and better than the rest of the auction sites.

INTRO TO THEMES - Themes are a great way for buyers and sellers to get together on cyrbid.

more from cyrbid Magazine...

Contact Us | Privacy | User Agreement

Northridge

http://www.ehammer.com

Create Auction | Classifieds | My Info   Sitemap | Help | Search | Auction Halls

THE ON-LINE AUCTION OF

Auction Categories

ANTIQUES & COLLECTIBLES

American Antiques
British and European Antiques
Asian Antiques
Artwork and Prints
Collectibles
Comic Books and Art
Ephemera
Photography
Pottery and Porcelain
Toys
Jewelry
more....

Welcome to eHammer

Search for Keywords:

[Search]

REGISTER
To
Buy and Sell

WHAT'S HOT
With
The Most Bids

AUCTION
Your
Own Item

TUTORIAL
To
Learn How

Premier Auctions

THE STING by AZMSEL

Black Ducks Limited Edition Print (e59)

Large and Impressive Spencerian Drawing

Colorful Still Life Theroum on Paper

Ty Series 3 trading cards-Unopened Case

DAVID WEBB ENAMEL,DIAMOND RING

DAVID WEBB EARRINGS - FABULOUS!!

Multi Spindled Morris Chair

Carved Folk Art Walking Stick with HAND

The Ingersell Family Portrait - NR!

1989 BMW 635 CSI 2 Door Coupe

EDDIE ARNING -GIRL WITH DOG...no reserve

1979 Volkswagon Convertible 11,700 Miles !

Beautiful 1890's Cutter Sled (e50)

Figurine and Shell Painting (c127)

eHammer Affiliates

Golden Lane Galleries

This Month's
Featured
Auction Hall

COMPANY
Come
and Browse
STORE

http://www.gomainline.com

Home Auctions Search Sellers Buyers Help Register Site map Log in Resources

Search

•The Collectible Experience!

Welcome!

Auction Categories

Register

Log In

Resources

List Items

Antiques (7)

Coins & Stamps (0)

Collectibles (116)

Comics (1830)

Dolls (20)

Jewelry & Watches (9)

Memorabilia (14)

Pottery & Glass (24)

Sports Cards/Memorabilia (47)

Toys (250)

All Auctions Listed... (21381)

Community Resources

News brought to you by:

Ask the Expert

Sellers Homepages

Collectors Calendar

Collecting Resources

Books/Magazines

Chat/ Message Boards

AntiqueHometowns

Mainline Radio Show Brought to you by:

Mainline Newsletters

Why Buy or Sell On Mainline?

Click Here to Bid by Phone

GoMainLine System Time   Company Information

http://www.haggle.com

The Go2Net Network ▾

AUCTIONS

Haggle Online

Register Here to buy and sell items

Something to Sell? start your auction here

Add Listing   Account Info   Rates   Search   Site Map   Help   About Haggle

Thousands of items open for bidding!

○ **Item Search**   [Search]

Haggle Time!
Featured items close on the hour, all times PST

Auction status: Closes Soon   Opened Recently   Closed Recently

Categories

Mon 02PM
Lotus Smartsuite *MILLENIUM EDITION ON CD* NO RESERVE TRUE AUCTION!
$9.99

Mon 03PM
Corel WordPerfect Office 2000 + $20.00 Bonus! NO RESERVE TRUE AUCTION!
$19.99

Mon 04PM
PC BLOWOUT 333Mhz/8MB AGP/32MB PC100/1MB Cache/ATX/SOUND/56K MODEM/10-100 NIC
$197.00

Tue 12AM
USED IOMEGA ZIP DISK 250MB $13.00

Tue 12AM
IOMEGA 250MB ZIP INTERNAL DRIVE IDE-OEM $116.00

Tue 01PM
OLIVETTI JP-192

Computers
PC-Desktops (114)
PC-Portables (64)
PC-Motherboards (77)
PC-Audio/Video (59)
PC-Controllers/etc. (26)
PC-Misc Hardware (109)
PC-Games (316)
PC-OS/Tools (152)
PC-Applications (315)
PC-Educational (343)
PC-Misc Software (230)
PC-Miscellaneous (43)
Mac-Desktops (20)
Mac-Portables (4)
Mac-Cards/Boards (5)
Mac-Software (64)
Mac-Miscellaneous (16)

Other Stuff
Consumer Electronics (34)
Photographic Equipment (31)
Services (16)
Business Equipment (15)
Home (40)
Automotive (31)
Sports/Recreation (61)
Collectibles (114)
Jewelry/Watches (129)
Toys/Fads (86)

More Computers
Workstations (3)
Other Systems (6)
PDAs/Organizers (5)
Game Systems (16)
Printers (28)
Monitors (33)
Multimedia (45)
Modems/ISDN (36)
Network (65)
Drives (189)
Input Devices (44)
Memory (20)
CPUs/Chips (65)
Misc Computer (39)
Internet Services (28)
Antique Computers (13)

Books (62)
Video (62)
Music (161)
Musical Instruments (7)
Tickets/Events (4)
Scientific/Engineering (4)
Miscellaneous (102)
Scams (8)
Firearms
Adults Only (297)

Top 10!

1. Intel P-III 500 Multi Media System w/ 20" SVGA Monitor BIDS START AT $1.00 WOW $700.00

2. MS OFFICE 97 PRO *** FULL VERSION *** CLEARANCE SALE ONLY $12.00

http://www.skybid.com

Categories

Antiques (5)
Boating (0)
Books, Movies, Music (2)
Coins & Stamps (0)
Collectibles (10)
Computers (0)
Software (0)
Dolls, Figures (0)
Jewelry, Gemstones (2)
Photo & Electronics (0)
Pottery & Glass (48)
Real Estate and Historic (0)
Sports Memorabilia (2)
Toys & Beanie Babies (0)
Miscellaneous (1)

SKYBID.COM Front Page Features

4 PCS. MAHOGANY BED SET

More features...

Extra! Extra!

EYE in the SKY! What's new and news at SkyBid.

- **LISTING FEES FROZEN** until further notice!
- SKYBID.COM NEARS 3000 USER MARK!
- **ATTENTION AOL USERS!!!**
- Welcome To SKYBID.COM!

QuikFacts

Total number of registered users: 2602

Current total number of listings: 70

Community Interest

Trivia
The keys on your keyboard are arranged to be in the most inconvenient configuration possible. The design was made in the mid 1800's to help stop manual typewriters from jamming due to quick typists. Think of that next time you're looking down at the keys!
Smiles
My next door neighbor picked all the green tomatoes in his garden to make room for the red ones.
Quotes
"Let us never negotiate out of fear, but let us never fear to negotiate."
John F. Kennedy

http://www.up4sale.com

Free Auctions Forever!

_____   GO

Advanced Search

Tip of the Day

You, too, can submit ideas for the Tip of The Day! If we select your tip, we'll put a link to your open auctions or comments page on our home page! Just click here to submit your idea for the tip of the day!

Hot Categories

Auctions Ending in Less Than 24 Hours
Toys
Action Figures
Beanie Babies®
Dolls
Holiday & Seasonal
Trading Cards
Software
Music
Comic Books

More Info

News Room
Links & Resources
AOL Guide
About Up4Sale

Monday, September 20, 1999 1:35:37 pm EDT

I'm Auction Amie
Welcome to Up4Sale Auctions We're working day and night to bring you the greatest auction experience on the web!

New Visitors - Click Here!   **Register Now!**

 Featured Auctions

Lips, Birthday Bear, Flitter No Reserve!	$60.25
How To Make A Fortune With Classified Ad	$5.00
Smokey The Bear Beanie	$12.00
Is This "the End" Black Bear Mwbmt??	$50.00
Fonecam Digital Camera With Modem	$100.00
White Stained Glass Light House Lamp	$19.00
New Blue Face Spangle In Hand No Reserve	$81.25
White Face Spangle - In Hand	$30.75
other featured auctions...	

Tip of the Day

Sellers! When responding to e-mailed comments or questions regarding one of your listings be calm, polite, and professional. Also express the desire to be of service in the future.

See auctions by
HAWKWAND

Submit a tip!

Home   Listings   Auction Item   Register   How To?   Member Center   Member Ratings

Visit eBay For More Great Items!

PRIORITY MAIL

Check out the US Postal Services Center!

http://auctions.yahoo.com

YAHOO! Auctions

Yahoo! - Account Info - Help

Welcome, Guest

Submit Item - My Auctions - Options - Sign in

Yahoo! Auctions

Getting Started
- Bidder Guide
- Seller Guide
- Community

You are not signed in
You must sign in to bid or sell.

Yahoo! ID: [ ]

Yahoo! Password: [ ]

☐ Remember my ID & Password

[Sign in]

New User?
Sign Up Here

Featured Category
- **Beanie Babies**
- **Jennifer Love Hewitt**
- **Tiger Woods**

Charity Auctions

Bid on **entertainment items** and **sports memorabilia** to benefit **A Nite to Unite.**

Other Charity Auctions
- Have dinner with **BILL COSBY** to support his high school
- Bid on **90210 Memorabilia** to support RAINN

Featured Auctions in Collector Plates

Hand Painted Floral Lefton Plate

Currier and Ives Plate, American Homestead Summer!

John Wayne High Country ** Mint Condition **

Find Auctions

[ ] [Search] Options

Antiques & Collectibles
(150,479)
Numismatics, Memorabilia, Porcelain...

Arts & Entertainment
(121,569)
Books, Music, Movies...

Business & Office *(3,712)*
Furniture, Fax Machines, Briefcases and Bags...

Clothing & Accessories
(48,635)
Jewelry, Women's, Men's...

Computers *(43,060)*
Hardware, Software, Domain Names...

Electronics & Cameras
(10,916)
Audio, Video, Cameras & Equipment...

Home & Garden *(24,120)*
Housewares, Baby Items, Furnishings...

Sports & Recreation *(45,317)*
Golf, Skiing & Snowboarding, Hobbies & Crafts...

Toys & Games *(184,100)*
Video Games, Furby, Beanie Babies@...

Trading Cards *(137,772)*
Baseball, Football, Games@...

Transportation *(4,019)*
Autos, Trucks, Motorcycles...

Other Goods & Services *(21,820)*
Hotels & Accommodations, Travel Tickets, Health & Beauty...

Specific Auctions

Specializing in certain items is not a new concept, and some of the online auction sites are doing it with success. Here is a sampling of a few...

http://www.auctionvine.com

Are fine and rare wines your weakness? Pay a visit to Auction Vine and acquire a bottle of Chateau Lynch-Bages Vintage 1961. This is not a 24 hour a day, 7 day a week auction and if there is no auction running when you visit you can sign up for an e-mail list that will keep you informed of upcoming site activities. There is also a mock auction where you can practice bidding before spending any actual money.

http://www.dollfans.com

This online auction is devoted to dolls and *Beanie Babies*, but the listings are scarce. Define scarce? There were a grand total of 10 listings, with nine beanie babies and one doll to be exact. The site offers other useful features though, including a doll collector forum and an online chat room.

http://www.justglass.com

Just glass is just that—glassware. The mission of this site is to replicate as nearly as possible the excitement and process of an actual vintage glass auction and they do just that. You might be surprised at how diverse a topic this is—anything from expensive art glass to glass marbles can be found here. Articles to upgrade your glass knowledge are offered, as is a chat room to "talk glass" with other members.

http://www.potteryauction.com

Did you guess pottery auction? Good for you! Categories are available offering anything from dinnerware to lamps, and individual pottery makers such as Rookwood, Stangl, Shawnee, Van Briggle, and Weller have their own categories. There is also a pottery chat room available from this auction site.

http://www.auctionvine.com

AUCTIONVINE
A Hobby Markets Auction Site

member of the

commerce network

Search

SmartFind™

Member Services

Help
Bid Status
Change Your Profile
Closed Auctions
Security/Privacy Policy
Recent Press
Our Merchant Partners
About Hobby Markets

Special Offers

Wine Consignments
Free E-mail Newsletters
Shop at Rare Wine Cellar
Magazine Subscriptions

The Collective Resource™

Currency Converter
Member Message Board
Set your Browser to AV

Other Auctions

Numismatists Online
SportsTrade
Philatelists Online

Welcome to AuctionVine, featuring the very best in Fine and Rare Wine Auctions on the Internet.

Results to the Morrell and Company auction that closed on 9/18: Part 1 (lots 1 to 275), Part 2 (lots 276 to 473), Part 3 (lots 474 to 859) and Part 4 (lots 860 to 1171).

View the Index to Morrell's current auction.

TO GO DIRECTLY TO A LOT IN THE MORRELL & COMPANY AUCTION

Enter a lot number: [ ] **submit**

Click on any auction banner listed below to view the lots available for bidding.

AuctionVine Presents

Morrell & Company Part 1
Closes 21-Oct-1999 06:00 PM PT (90 Lots)

(Lots 1-90) The Following Fine Collection Of California Cabernet Sauvignon And Vintage Ports Was Assembled By A Southern Gentleman During The 1980ís. The Collection Is A Combination Of Wines Purchased On Release From The Wineries And The Major Auction Houses In San Francisco, Chicago And London. Featured In The Collection Are A Number Of Large Format Bottles Including Several Balthazars, A Range Of Artist Labels, And Fabulously Etched Designs.

Morrell & Company Charity Champagnes
Closes 21-Oct-1999 09:00 PM PT (70 Lots)

http://www.dollfans.com

The *premier* resource for Doll Collectors worldwide!

Sponsored by: Queen of Hearts Collectibles and SpiderWare.

Visit www.barbiefans.com and www.beaniefans.com for more collectibles fun!

**Julie Good-Kruger LE 50 Exclusive Doll
available from Queen of Hearts!**

Please Register with us to get regular updates on current events, news and conferences in the collector doll world!

You can Quick Register with just one click!

Email: [ ]

[Do it!]

Also, Please sign our guestbook!

Enter Doll Collectors Forums to interact with other doll collectors!

http://www.justglass.com

No Listing Fees or Commissions

@ JUST GLASS

Welcome
About Us
News Events
TV/Audio Page
Press Releases
Site Map

RESOURCES

Newsletter
Reference Library
Dealer Shops
The Bookstore
Links

CONNECTIONS

Do You ICQ?
Join Our IE
Channel

CATEGORIES

Art Glass *(23)*
American *(10)*
Bohemian *(3)*
Czech *(2)*
English *(1)*
General *(2)*
Italian *(3)*

Carnival Glass *(2)*
General *(1)*
Vintage Carnival *(1)*

Coll. 40's, 50's, 60's Glass
(10)

Contemporary Glass
(1970 - Present) *(13)*

Depression Glass *(12)*

Elegant Depression Glass
(142)
Cambridge *(9)*
Duncan Miller *(14)*
Fostoria *(54)*
General *(22)*
Heisey *(7)*

Tiffin *(10)*

Fenton *(15)*

Fire-King / Anchor
Hocking *(12)*

Glass Animals *(9)*

Glass Bottles *(1)*

Glass Jewelry *(2)*

Glass Ornaments *(5)*

Glass Paper/Books
(2)

Kitchen Glass *(7)*

Lamps / Lighting *(4)*

Milk Glass *(2)*

Misc. Glass *(10)*

New Glass *(2)*

Opalescent Glass *(3)*

Paperweights *(30)*

Perfume Bottles *(13)*

Phoenix /
Consolidated *(35)*

Pottery

Vaseline Glass *(2)*

http://www.potteryauction.com

pottery auction

| HOME | REGISTER | SELLERS | BROWSE | SITEMAP | HELP | SEARCH |

Featuring....

American Art Pottery

NEW MEMBERS
REGISTER HERE
SUCCESS STORIES
FEEDBACK
SITE MAP
HELP
FAQs
FORGOT PASSWORD?
FEATURED AUCTIONS
ENDING TODAY
NEW TODAY
JUST GLASS

Welcome
to
The World's First Pottery
Auction Community

List
List An Item

Register
Register Here!

Chat
Chat in our
Coffee Shop
& Bookstore

Categories
Pottery Categories

as seen on
shopnow.com

Online Malls

In addition, there are sites where merchandise is for sale by a set price rather than in an auction environment. Some of these sites also deserve your attention.

American Antique Mall
http://www.elegantantiques.com

American Antiques Mall offers a selection of antiques and collectibles in online antique dealer booths. Primarily, the offerings are Depression glass and pottery.

Antique Alley
http://www.bmark.com/aa/

Over 100 independent dealers, each with an online catalog, a search engine to help you locate what you're looking for, and a comprehensive directory of traditional antique shops with their snail-mail addresses.

collect.com
http://www.csmonline.com/buysell/

Thousands of items offered by hundreds of merchants. Browse categories or search by keyword(s).

Collector Online
http://www.collectoronline.com

A major Internet mall, with over 200 dealers. An innovative online Inventory Management System (IMS) allows you to catalog an unlimited number of items and send them to eBay™, Yahoo! Auctions, or your Collector Online booth with the click of a mouse.

GoUniq.com
http://www.gouniq.com

Multiple dealers with fixed prices.

Ruby Lane
http://www.rubylane.com

An excellent antiques and collectibles search engine, as well as a place to build your online storefront and display your merchandise for sale.

http://www.tias.com

Shop   **Sell**   **Talk**   **Learn**   **News**   **Respond.com**   **Feedback**   **Help**

"Come buy and sell with us..."

SEARCH

Type in keyword(s) and click "search" to find a particular item. If you need help refining your search method, please see our Search Tips page. For more directed searching use Advanced Search.

| Search | Over 161118 items for sale!

BROWSE BY CATEGORY

Select a category from the menu below and click "Jump". Additional subcategories will be presented to further direct your search.

To pick a category, click here. ▾ | Jump | Over 600 total categories!

WHAT'S NEW

Wednesday, October 20 1999

Squirrel Haven's Antiques and Collectibles Many new items added at Squirrel Haven. Enjoy a 10% discount on all dolls. Have fun.

G P S F Antiques GPSF Antiques has added 3 Autograph related items(Alloysius Derso-Political Illustrator, Marechal Petain of France, Telegram Harry S Truman), 6 Philatelic items, a Monograph and Cigarette Card catalog.

Marion Antiques And Collectibles A rare and wonderful piece of Lefton history is now available! Take a minute and check it out. And thanks for stopping by.

The Internet Antique Store
http://www.tias.com

One of the largest antiques and collectibles malls on the Internet. Links to over 190 dealers and a search engine make shopping fun and easy.

Individual Dealers

Some of the finest antiques you'll find on the Internet are available from a handful of top-notch individual dealers.

A-Mark Precious Metals
http://www.amark.com

Since its founding in 1965, A-Mark has grown into a firm with annual sales exceeding $1 billion and is a full service precious metal trading company offering a wide array of products and services. Daily prices are posted for gold, silver and other precious metals.

Hakes Americana & Collectibles
http://www.hakes.com

Hakes mail order auctions are well known in the collectibles trade, and many of the same fine items are available online at fixed prices.

D'Antiques Limited
http://www.dantiques.com

Don't be fooled by the D'Antiques claim of being the premiere virtual junk store on the Web—they have some fine antiques and collectibles too.

Durwyn Smedley Antiques
http://www.smedley.com

Modern design movements of the 20th Century including Arts & Crafts, Art Deco, and Mid-Century Modern. Art pottery and tiles, American designer dinnerware.

Funk and Junk
http://www.funkandjunk.com

Character glasses, action figures, five-and-dime items, political items, vintage clothing, and much more including categories by decades (1950s, 1970s, etc.)

Old Orchard Antiques
http://www.oldorchardantiques.com
A selection of advertising, ephemera, jewelry, glass, pottery, and toys coupled with friendly, efficient service makes this a site to bookmark.

Southampton Antiques
(http://www.souhantq.com)
Based in Massachusetts, Southampton has a wonderful selection of fine quality antiques. Their Web site is well designed, attractive, easy to navigate, and contains some great New England finds.

Information Directories
Looking for links to other antiques and collectibles sites, price guides, and reference books? Look no further.

Antique Hot Spots
http://www.antiquehotspots.com
A directory of hundreds of antique and collectibles sites with links to them from one location. You'll find links to anything from online auctions to individual shops to companies where you can buy display showcases.

collect.com
http://www.csmonline.com
Subscribe to the Antique Trader online price guide, plan your next trip with a show and auction calendar, purchase price guides and reference books, join discussion groups, all from one source.

Curioscape
http://www.curioscape.com
A directory of links to specific categories, including art, coins, dolls, glassware, and many more.

Collector Link (Cards)
http://www.collector-link.com
Web sites and news groups for card magazines and price guides, card issuers, dealers and private collectors.

ShopNow.com
http://www.shopnow.com

While this is a site that lists stores of all descriptions, not just antiques and collectibles, all you have to do is type "antiques" or "collectibles" into the Easy-Search box on their home page, click "Find It", and get a list of links to more fun places to explore.

World Collectors Net
http://www.worldcollectorsnet.com

A site for collectibles, featuring a shopping arcade, information pages, articles, reviews, message boards, price guides, a bookstore and a swap shop all under one virtual roof.

http://www.amark.com

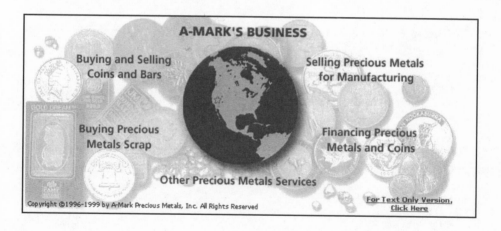

http://www.hakes.com

Auction 155 is Now Open - for a FREE copy of our Auction Catalogue email us

Hake's Americana & Collectibles
P.O. Box 1444 ~ York, PA 17405
(717) 848-1333
Business Hours for Phone Calls: 10 a.m. to 5 p.m.
Eastern. Monday-Friday
(Except Auction Closing Nights)
info@hakes.com

Auctioneers, Publishers, Consultants and Appraisers of all Artifacts of Popular Culture

Click below on the link of your choice

- Future Auction Schedule

- Immediate Sale Highlights

- Price Guides by Ted Hake

- 1000s of Items for Sale Now

- Hake's Want List

- History of Hake's Americana

- Related Links

Collectibles Priced for Immediate Sale

http://www.dantiques.com

Welcome to D'Antiques, Ltd.

The premier virtual junk store on the Web

About Dan and Marilyn.
Free Collectors Resources!

Product Catalog

Search Product Catalog
By Product Name
By Maker
By Artists
Recently Added
Browse by category

Direct To Most Popular Categories
Board Games
Ceramics
Video Games
Electronics

Top Level Categories

Advertising	*Automotive*	*Bottles and Openers*	*Boxes*	*Breweriana*	*Calculating Devices*
Ceramics	*Clocks*	*Clothing and Accessories*	*Disney*	*Electronics*	*Ephemera*
Fairs/Expositions	*Fine Arts/Furniture*	*Fraternal Organizations*	*Games*	*General*	*Holidays*
Jewelry and Silver	*Kitchen*	*Laboratory*	*Lunch Boxes and Picnic*	*Militaria*	*Musical Instruments*
Occupied Japan	*Pens and Desk Items*	*Petroliana*	*Photographica*	*Politics*	*Railroadiana*
Recordings	*Rock and Roll*	*Science Fiction/ Fantasy*	*Soft Drinks*	*Sports*	*TV, Radio, Movies*
Technical Items, General	*Tins*	*Tobaccoianna*	*Tools*	*Toys*	*Trays*

http://www.smedley.com

smedley.com

Hosting antique dealers and 20th Century dealers of the highest quality

Durwyn Smedley 20th Century
Modern design movements of the 20th Century including Arts & Crafts; Art Deco; Mid-Century Modern; upscale, designer 50's. Art pottery and tile from all eras, American designer dinnerware. First Indiana antique shop on the World Wide Web.

Red Goose Antiques
Muncie Pottery, American and European art pottery, Fiesta, Laughlin Art China, and a general line of antiques

webmaster@smedley.com - Site feedback and bug reports
info@smedley.com - Site design and hosting information

The URL of this site: http://www.smedley.com

http://www.funkandjunk.com

OLD ORCHARD

Advertising	Ephemera	Toys, Sports	Glassware

Jewelry, Purses	Clocks, Metals	China, Pottery

Welcome to the Old Orchard Antiques Home Page.
We have many fine antiques and collectibles to suit your collecting tastes.

Visit us at the ETC Antiques Station in scenic Wellsboro, PA.-
Home of the " Pennsylvania Grand Canyon".

WELCOME

SOUTHAMPTON ANTIQUES

Southampton Antiques has the largest selection of antique American, Victorian, and turn of the century furniture in the Northeast. Items are offered in both "as found" and restored condition.

We are proud to present our catalogue and invite you to browse through the collection of over 200 still and VIDEO images (QTVR).
The shop is open Saturday 10:00 - 5:00 or by appointment.
Closed August.

Antique Hot Spots

#..A..B..C..D..E..F..G..H..I..J..K..L..M..N..O..P..Q..R..S..T..U..V..W..X..Y..Z

Antique Hot Spots' Favorite Trading Place:
Over 2,500,000 antiques, collectibles and more.

Book Store: Reference Books on Antiques and Collectibles

Banner Advertising Information

Hot Site: Antique Hot Spot's Featured Site

Keyword Search on Antique Hot Spots!   NEW

List Your Site: Very Easy With The New Form.

Question Board: Do You Have The Answer?

Wanted Board: Do You Have The Item?

Web Site: Antique Hot Spots For Sale

Yip! Yip! Yip! Antiques and Collectibles For Sale

dv@antiquehotspots.com

Counter Posted 4/15/98 35080
Fast Counter Information

THE PRICE OF LIBERTY IS ETERNAL VIGILANCE!

http://www.csmonline.com

Home | Buy/Sell | Online Price Guides | Reference | Forums | Collect.com Network

Home Page   Search [   ] Go   Site Navigation ▼ Go

CONTENTS

Buy/Sell
Merchandise
Classifieds
Web Pages
Quarter Trading

Online Price Guides
Antique Trader
Beans! Magazine
Tuff Stuff

Reference
Books
Magazines
Calendars
Directories
News

Forums

About Collect.com
Advertise
FAQ
Contact Us

| What's New Today, October 20, 1999 |
| No "data" parameter specified. |
| No "data" parameter specified |

Welcome to **Collect.com** - The Premier Online Antiques & Collectibles Community. Formerly *Collector's Super Mall*, we have added many new features to benefit buyers and sellers alike! Within Collect.com, you can:

- Begin your own Interactive Web Site
- Place your own online Classified Ads. **NEW! We've added several thousand more ads from leading antique and collectible publications!**
- Access the Internet's most comprehensive Online Price Guide
- Post events in our Show & Auction Calendar
- Subscribe to many quality publications
- Purchase price guides and reference books
- Join in Discussion Forums for almost any topic
- Search or browse our up-to-date News features
- And much, much more!

So be sure to spend some time within our site and take full advantage of all the benefits that Collect.com has to offer.

FEATURES

News Library

Register to view the hundreds of news, information and feature articles available in the News Reference Library!

Collect.com Network
Antique & Collectables
Antique Journal
Antique Trader
Antique Trader Books
Atlantique City
Beans! Magazine
Big Reel
Collector Magazine
Cotton & Quail
Discoveries
Kovels
Krause Publications
Military Trader
Ohio Antique Review
Postcard Collector
Tuff Stuff

http://www.curioscape.com

POTTERY BID

Curioscape
www.curioscape.com

The Internet's Exclusive
Antiquing & Collecting Directory

s e a r c h ! - (Find something CREEPY? Enter **Halloween**)

[Enter!] **Advanced Search**

b r o w s e ! - Sites and Shops from these categories!

A better SITE-MAP! NEW!

Visit the one and only "Silver Slug", the ferry Kalakala in Seattle this Summer!

Art
Paintings,Crafts,Photographs
Auctions
On-line
Books
Comics,Mags,Rare,Used
Business
Antique Shops, Auctions,Announcements
Cards
Sport Cards, Post Cards, Phone Cards
Classic Machinery
Automotive, Aviation, Boating, Tractors
Coins
Tokens, Medals, Paper Money, Casino Chips
Devices
Cameras, Clocks, Radio, Tools
Decorative
Baskets, Dept 56, Figurines
Dolls
Barbie, Porcelain, Plush, Teddy Bears

Entertainment
Movies, Music, TV, RadioShows,Autographs
Events
Fairs, Shows, Swap Meets, Tours
Glass
Carnival, Crystal, Depression Glass
Household Items
Appliances, Furnishings, Desktop, Clothing
Jewelry
Rings, Necklaces, Pins
Memorabilia
Baseball, Basketball, Other Sports
Militaria
Civil War, World Wars, Uniforms, Guns, Medals
Miscellaneous
Unique & Odd ball Stuff
Music
Vinyl Records, CDs, ...
Old Advertising
Paper & Ephemera, Bottles, Products

Paper & Ephemera
Advertising, Books,Cards, Posters
Pottery & Ceramics
Royal Doulton, Roseville, Fiesta, Hummel
Resources
Directories, Guides, Lost & Found
Wanted To Buy Lists
Scientific
Insulators, Rocks, Metals, Fossils
Shops
United States, European,....
Stamps
Various·Countries,Day Covers,Resources
Style & Cultural
Advertising, Smokerama, Disney,
Sci-Fi, Western Style
Table Settings
Dishware, Glass, Silver, S&P Shakers
Toys
Action-Figures, Die Cast, Miniatures, Beanies®

http://www.collector-link.com

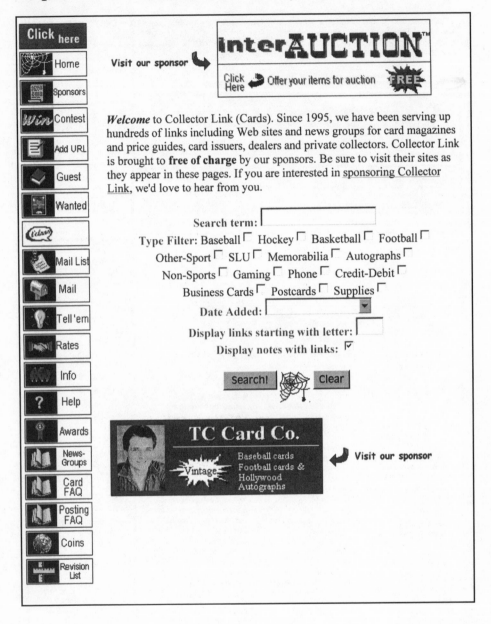

Visit our sponsor → interAUCTION™
Click Here → Offer your items for auction FREE

Navigation buttons:
- Click here
- Home
- Sponsors
- Win Contest
- Add URL
- Guest
- Wanted
- Mail List
- Mail
- Tell 'em
- Rates
- Info
- Help
- Awards
- News-Groups
- Card FAQ
- Posting FAQ
- Coins
- Revision List

Welcome to Collector Link (Cards). Since 1995, we have been serving up hundreds of links including Web sites and news groups for card magazines and price guides, card issuers, dealers and private collectors. Collector Link is brought to **free of charge** by our sponsors. Be sure to visit their sites as they appear in these pages. If you are interested in sponsoring Collector Link, we'd love to hear from you.

Search term: [   ]

Type Filter: Baseball □ Hockey □ Basketball □ Football □
Other-Sport □ SLU □ Memorabilia □ Autographs □
Non-Sports □ Gaming □ Phone □ Credit-Debit □
Business Cards □ Postcards □ Supplies □

Date Added: [▼]

Display links starting with letter: [   ]
Display notes with links: ☑

[Search!]   [Clear]

TC Card Co.
Vintage
Baseball cards
Football cards &
Hollywood
Autographs
→ **Visit our sponsor**

http://www.shopnow.com

shopnow.com
connecting buyers and sellers worldwide

search for: stores ● products ○
Type in a store or item and we'll help you find it.

go!

- stores
- gifts
- products
- auctions
- your town
- freebies

Shop the Mall

The ShopNow.com mall conveniently connects you with over 30,000 merchants in 28 categories.

You're only a click away from all your favorite stuff!

join now!

join ShopNow.com

store of the week

eBay

featured stores

eBatts.com
Damark International
800.com
toysmart.com
Florist.com

hot bargains

Austin Powers!
Qwest - 5¢ per minute
Halloween Deals
"Yo Quiero" Dog!
Cool Body Art

Business Tools

CommerceTrust
Merchant Center
List Your Store
Syndicate Partners

ShopNow.com Customer Support 1 800 SHOPNOW

My Favorites | MyShopNow | Contact Us | New to the site?
Advertise With Us | Merchant Center | Privacy Policy | About Our Company
Investor Information | Unlimited Career Opportunities

powered by
commercetrust.com
© 1999, ShopNow.com Inc.

http://www.worldcollectorsnet.com

World Collectors Net
'the collecting portal'

World Collectors Net
"by collectors for collectors"

- Shopping Arcade
- Collectibles Featured
- OnLine Magazine
- Message Boards
- Price Guides & Trends
- Links Directory
- Collectibles News
- Bookstore
- Contact Us
- SURVEY

Welcome to the **World Collectors Net**, the Web's #1 meeting place for Collectors. Throughout our pages, you will find information and features on dozens of popular collectibles, including our free interactive Message Boards and OnLine Magazine. **WCN** is created *by* Collectors *for* Collectors. Enjoy!

Search

Latest News
From the world of collecting

New Collectibles
* Robert Tonner Dolls
* PEZ
* Artesania Rinconada
* Batman
* Just the Right Shoe
* Breyer Horses

SWAP SHOP
Buy, sell and trade with collectors world-wide

WCN **Collectibles Shopping Arcade**

Featuring collectible creators, manufacturers, shops, clubs & magazines from all over the world.

New Members
Crystal Reef
Modern Icons
First Fax 2000
Designs by Milford

Magazine
Online magazine

Collectibles Directory
Search the web for collectible sites

auction universe

WCN

Cardew Design

Amyot & Watt

PROTECT

MESSAGE BOARDS
Over 80 collecting message boards

October Contest #2

CHAPTER 5

Using eBay™, the Granddaddy of the Online Auctions

We've finally arrived! This chapter will walk you through the process of registering and using eBay™, the world's largest online auction. I'll stay basic here but give you some advanced tips in Chapter 7. Once you've mastered the skills associated with using eBay™ you can visit any auction you'd like-they all work very similarly.

The functions described in this chapter can be accessed from eBay's™ home page **(www.ebay.com)** or once you're inside the eBay™ community from the menu at the top of each screen. If you're having trouble finding a particular area within eBay™ click Site Map on the menu and you'll have access to links from all areas of the eBay™ community. So let's GO!

Register

If you're 18 years of age or older and have a permanent address and e-mail account you can register to use eBay™. Registration is a process that requires submitting (online, of course) some basic information and receiving back a confirmation number via e-mail. You then confirm your registration by accepting eBay's™ User Agreement and choosing a screen name and password (do NOT use the confirmation number eBay™ sent to you for a password). This information is again submitted online, along with the original confirmation number supplied by eBay™, and your registration is complete. eBay™ does a good job of walking you through the process, making it very easy. In fact the hardest part is figuring out what you want to call yourself (your eBay™ screen name) and choosing a password. Don't forget that password! It's your ticket to the eBay™ community.

Registration is a one-time occurrence and once confirmed you may sell or buy as much as you'd like without doing it again. Depending on the volume of users the wait to get your confirmation e-mail might take hours or perhaps a day, so if you register and want to bid right away you may be disappointed. But while you're waiting for your confirmation e-mail you can browse the listings and get familiar with the auction community in general.

You will notice that eBay™ now gives you the option of registering using *SSL*. SSL stands for Secure Sockets Layer and is a technology developed by Netscape (don't panic-it works with Microsoft Internet Explorer too) as a more secure way of sending information over the Internet. While the registration process does not require you to give any more information than is already available in public records, I recommend you always use SSL when available for any Internet transactions. Online privacy will become more of an issue, and you should get in the habit of using any means available to protect yours.

To register using SSL, simply click the box as instructed on the eBay™ Registration screen and then click the **Begin registration process now** bar. A popup box will appear saying that you are about to view pages over a secure connection. Click **OK** and you will proceed to the secure registration site. Check the address bar at the top of your browser window-if it starts with https:// instead of http:// you are on a secure site. Another way to verify you're secure is to check for an icon in the lower right part of your browser window that looks like a locked padlock.

BUYERS

Other than the money you'll owe the seller when purchasing an item, buying on eBay™ is free. There are no fees to pay as there are when listing an item for sale.

Browsing the listings

If you're not looking for anything in particular (if you are see Search listings) you can browse through thousands of listings and most assuredly find something of interest to you. eBay™ is split into over 2,000 categories, and while this alone sounds intimidating it makes browsing much easier than if everything was together. You can choose categories from Antiques to Computers to Jewelry. Once you select a category you can refine even more; for instance Antiques lets you choose Ancient World, Books & Manuscripts, Folk Art, and others. Click on a category and the listings appear before you, ready for you to place your bids!

eBay™ Registration Screen

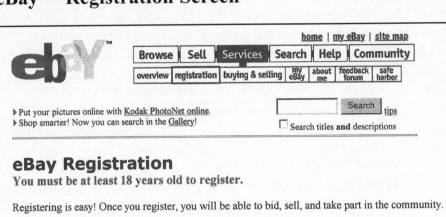

home | my eBay | site map

Browse | Sell | Services | Search | Help | Community

overview | registration | buying & selling | my eBay | about me | feedback forum | safe harbor

▸ Put your pictures online with Kodak PhotoNet online.
▸ Shop smarter! Now you can search in the Gallery!

Search | tips

☐ Search titles **and** descriptions

eBay Registration

You must be at least 18 years old to register.

Registering is easy! Once you register, you will be able to bid, sell, and take part in the community.

To begin, please tell us which country you live in by selecting from the list below.

> United States
> APO/FPO
> Canada
> United Kingdom
> Afghanistan
> Albania
> Algeria
> American Samoa
> Andorra
> Angola

☐ Click on the box to the left if you prefer to register using *SSL*.

After you've selected the country you live in, click the button below.

Begin the registration process now

Announcements | Register | eBay Store | SafeHarbor | Feedback Forum | About eBay
Home | My eBay | Site Map

Browse | Sell | Services | Search | Help | Community
Overview | Register | Buy and Sell | My eBay | About Me Login | Feedback Forum | Safeharbor

Copyright © 1995-1999 eBay Inc. All Rights Reserved.
Designated trademarks and brands are the property of their respective owners.
Use of this Web site constitutes acceptance of the eBay User Agreement and Privacy
Policy.

eBay™ Registration Screen (con't)

home | my eBay | site map

Browse	Sell	Services	Search	Help	Community

overview	registration	buying & selling	my eBay	about me	feedback forum	safe harbor

eBay Registration

If you're not from the United States, click here.

How to Register - To register on eBay, follow the registration process below. When you complete all three steps, you can begin buying and selling on eBay.

1) Complete the eBay Initial Registration Form - Simply fill out the registration form below, review your information for accuracy, and click the Submit button.

2) Receive Confirmation Instructions - eBay will send you an e-mail message with a confirmation code.
If you already have completed step 1 and you need eBay to resend your confirmation instructions click here.

3) Confirm Your Registration - Once you have your access code (and your e-mail address), finalize your registration by accepting the eBay User Agreement and complete the eBay Confirm your Registration form.
If you have your confirmation code and you are ready to confirm your registration, click here.

Please Note: To be eligible to register, you must be over 18 years of age and provide valid contact information, including a valid e-mail address. **eBay** will not use any registration information for marketing, nor will we disclose this information to any outside party.

If you would like to read a full explanation of our privacy policy, click on the TRUSTe button below:

Step 1 - eBay Initial Registration Form

Simply fill out the information below and click the **continue** button.
Required entries are shown in **green**.

E-mail address e.g, username@aol.com	_____ (required) *Note:* AOL and WebTV Users: Please remove any spaces from your username and add the domain suffix (@aol.com or @webtv.net to your username). For example, if your username is joecool, your e-mail address would be joecool@aol.com

eBay™ Registration Screen (con't)

Full name e.g., John H. Doe	[_____] (required) First M. Last
Company	[_____] (optional)
Address	[_____] (required)
City	[_____] (required)
State	[Select State ▾] (required)
Zip Code	[_____] (required)
Primary phone # e.g., (408) 555 - 1234	([____]) [____] - [____] (required) [____] (extension)
Secondary phone #	([____]) [____] - [____] (optional) [____] (extension)
Fax #	([____]) [____] - [____] (optional)

Optional Info	
How did you first hear about eBay?	[Select here ▾]
If you have a promotional priority code, please enter it:	[____] - [____] - [____]
If a friend referred you to eBay, please enter your friend's email address:	[_____] We can only accept e-mail addresses (i.e., ebayfriend@aol.com)
Do you use eBay for personal or business purposes?	[Select here ▾]
I am most interested in:	Not Selected Antiques (pre-1900) Collectibles Computers Memorabilia
Age	[Select an age range ▾]
Education	[Select an education ▾]
Annual Household Income	[Select an income range ▾]

eBay™ Antiques Page

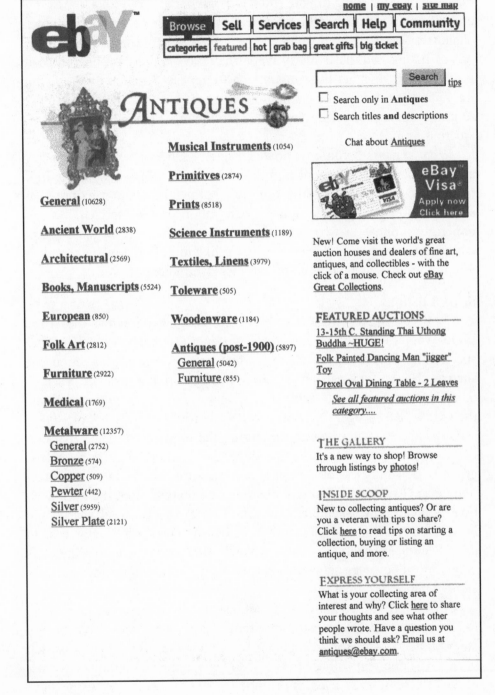

home | my ebay | site map

Browse | **Sell** | **Services** | **Search** | **Help** | **Community**

categories | featured | hot | grab bag | great gifts | big ticket

☐ Search only in **Antiques**
☐ Search titles **and** descriptions

Chat about <u>Antiques</u>

ANTIQUES

General (10628)

Ancient World (2838)

Architectural (2569)

Books, Manuscripts (5524)

European (850)

Folk Art (2812)

Furniture (2922)

Medical (1769)

Metalware (12357)
  General (2752)
  Bronze (574)
  Copper (509)
  Pewter (442)
  Silver (5959)
  Silver Plate (2121)

Musical Instruments (1054)

Primitives (2874)

Prints (8518)

Science Instruments (1189)

Textiles, Linens (3979)

Toleware (505)

Woodenware (1184)

Antiques (post-1900) (5897)
  General (5042)
  Furniture (855)

eBay™ Visa®
Apply now
Click here

New! Come visit the world's great auction houses and dealers of fine art, antiques, and collectibles - with the click of a mouse. Check out <u>eBay Great Collections</u>.

FEATURED AUCTIONS
13-15th C. Standing Thai Uthong Buddha ~HUGE!
Folk Painted Dancing Man "jigger" Toy
Drexel Oval Dining Table - 2 Leaves
See all featured auctions in this category....

THE GALLERY
It's a new way to shop! Browse through listings by <u>photos</u>!

INSIDE SCOOP
New to collecting antiques? Or are you a veteran with tips to share? Click <u>here</u> to read tips on starting a collection, buying or listing an antique, and more.

EXPRESS YOURSELF
What is your collecting area of interest and why? Click <u>here</u> to share your thoughts and see what other people wrote. Have a question you think we should ask? Email us at <u>antiques@ebay.com</u>.

Viewing a listing

Scroll through the myriad of listings in your category and find one that sounds interesting to you. If it has a green icon that looks like a camera in front of it you're in luck-the seller has supplied a photo of the merchandise. But don't be dismayed if it doesn't-sellers use different methods of listing and, particularly when they have more than one photo to post, don't always get the camera icon to appear. So click on the listing that interests you and hope a photo is there. If it's not, I recommend you refrain from bidding (see Chapter 8-Protecting Yourself from Internet Auction Fraud).

What appears before you now is a screen showing some information about the seller, the current high bid amount for this auction, the high bidder's screen name and the time left before the auction expires. By scrolling down you come upon a description of the merchandise and hopefully a photo or two. Scrolling even further you're in the bid area where you can specify the amount you'd like to bid on this merchandise. The minimum acceptable bid is also displayed here.

Search listings

While the Internet has search engines that spread across the World Wide Web, some online auctions have engines that search their sites specifically. These are invaluable when browsing a large auction site such as eBay™ for a particular item or item group. For instance, a search of eBay™ on October 9, 1999 at 2:45 p.m. EST for listings containing the words "Roy Rogers" yielded no less than 951 entries! (As an interesting aside, the same search run during the production of the first edition of this book, a year earlier, produced 377 entries. eBay™ has indeed grown!) Belt buckles, autographs, posters, slippers and just about anything else "Roy Rogers" was available to be bought-all at the same auction. You can now assemble a collection in less than a week that would have taken years and possibly a lifetime before. Does this take the fun out of collecting? Absolutely not, as you'll find out when your heart is pounding as you wait to see if your bid on an item you've always wanted holds up in the final minutes.

eBay™ provides a number of useful search programs. You can search for items by title, items listed by a particular seller, items you (or any other bidder) has bid on recently, or by the number eBay™ assigns each listing. The one you will use the most, at least in the beginning, is by title.

A title search, as used with online auctions, works by using keywords. Click the **Search** menu at the top of your eBay™ screen, type in

Browsing an eBay™ Listing

home | my eBay | site map

| Browse | Sell | Services | Search | Help | Community |

Item view

4th Gene Convention Doll-Best Package on eBay
Item #183593457
Dolls, Figures:Dolls:Fashion (Non-Barbie):Gene

Description →

Bid! →

Currently	**$355.00**		First bid	**$50.00**
Quantity	1		# of bids	**12** (bid history) (with emails)
Time left	**5 days, 1 hours +**		Location	**Western Maryland**
Started	10/17/99, 18:40:26 PDT		✉ (mail this auction to a friend)
Ends	10/24/99, 18:40:26 PDT		🎁 (request a gift alert)
Seller	**antiqueray** (411) ⭐ m☺			
	(view comments in seller's Feedback Profile) (view seller's other auctions)			
	(ask seller a question)			
High bid	**aanastasi** (55) ☆			
Payment	Visa/MasterCard, Money Order/Cashiers Checks, Personal Checks			
Shipping	Buyer pays actual shipping charges, Seller might ship to home country only. See item description for details			

Seller assumes all responsibility for listing this item. You should contact the seller to resolve any questions before bidding. Currency is U.S. dollar ($) unless otherwise noted.

Description

4th Gene Convention Doll-Best Package on eBay

"Mood Music" Gene-limited edition of 800 for the 4th Gene Convention, Oct. 15-16, 1999 in Cherry Hill, NJ. Never out of the box. She comes with a print of the artists' original drawing, a letter from the Gene team, AND the certificate is signed by Lynne Day, the costume designer for this doll. Other goodies from the convention package

---

what you're looking for, and click the **Search** button. If you are looking for a specific group of words that must fall in the exact order you type them, like the Roy Rogers example above, remember to enclose the words in quotes.

You can narrow your response by first visiting a specific category. When you visit the listings page of a specific category you will see a Search box at the top right of the screen. You will also see below the search box that you have the option of running the search only within that

eBay™ Search Page

Browse | **Sell** | **Services** | Search | **Help** | **Community**

find items | find members | personal shopper

▶ Put your pictures online with **Kodak PhotoNet online**.
▶ Shop smarter! Now you can search in the **Gallery**!

[ ] Search [ ] tips

☐ Search titles **and** descriptions

Find Items

By Title - By Item Number - By Seller - By Bidder - Completed Search - International Search

By Title eBay's most popular search feature	[ ] Search tips ☐ Search title **and** description
Category	All Categories ▾
Price Range	Between $ [ ] And $ [ ]
Regions	All of eBay ▾ or Search by country
Order by	Ending Date ▾ ◉ ascending ○ descending
View Results	◉ All items ○ All items with Gallery preview NEW! ○ Gallery items only NEW! ☐ Text only results
	Search completed auctions

By Item Number Use only if you have the item number (#)	Item Number (#) [ ] Search

By Seller Find all items currently listed by a specific seller	[ ] Search User ID or email address of seller. See your favorite seller's listings.
Include bidder emails	◉ No ○ Yes
Include completed items	◉ No ○ All ○ Last Day ○ Last 2 Days ○ Last Week ○ Last 2 Weeks

category. This is immensely helpful when using keywords with more than one possible meaning, for instance the last name of a particular artist. If you could not narrow your search to a particular category, the search would return results in any auction that found the name. This could include sports figures on trading cards, brand names, etc.

Here's an example. I ran a search on prints by artist R. Atkinson Fox, first running a general search of the entire eBay™ site for just the word Fox. It returned 2684 auctions, most of which had nothing to do with R. Atkinson Fox. By going to the Antiques: Prints category first and running the search from there, specifying to search only in that category, only 69 items were returned-the vast majority of them actually being R. Atkinson Fox prints.

Bidding

Hold onto your wallet, it's time to bid! New users tend to find this addicting at first, so it's a good rule to set yourself a spending limit before you start and stick to it. Bidding at an online auction is the same as entering into a legal contract with the seller, so be prepared to go through with your purchase if you bid. Otherwise you'll find yourself with negative feedback (see Chapter 7—Advanced tips).

Once you've arrived at the description page of the item you want to bid on, either click on the bid paddle or scroll to the bottom of the page to get to the bidding section. Here you will see a form where you must input the maximum amount you are willing to bid. Enter a number, without dollar signs but using a decimal in the appropriate place, and click **Review Bid**. Another screen will display where can review the bid you are about to place and enter your eBay™ User ID and password. Enter them and click **Place Bid**. You're on your way.

eBay™ works with a system known as Proxy Bidding, which is difficult to explain but once you've used it a bit I think you'll understand why it's done and will like it. Proxy bidding means you may place a bid as high as you'd like and the bid amount will only jump as high as needed to surpass the previous high bidder. The higher bid you made is protected and used only if another bidder tries to surpass you. Here are some possible scenarios…

1. You've just found a 19th century quilt you like, and the current high bid is $135. You are willing to bid up to $225 for this item. You place your bid at $225 and are notified that you are now the high bidder and the next acceptable bid is $155. You scroll down to view the

Placing a Bid on eBay™

Bidding

4th Gene Convention Doll-Best Package on eBay (Item #183593457)

Current bid	$355.00
Bid increment	$5.00
Minimum bid	**$360.00**

Registration required. eBay requires registration in order to bid. Find out how to <u>become a registered user</u>. It's fast and it's **free**!

To finalize your bid, you will need to submit your User ID and Password in the next step — once you click on Review Bid.

[_____] *Current minimum bid is 360.00*

Enter your maximum bid
- Remember to type in **numbers only** and use a decimal point (.) when necessary. **Don't include a currency symbol ($) or thousand separator.** For example: 1000000.00

Bid efficiently with Proxy Bidding — here's how it works:
- Your maximum bid is kept secret, and **it's not necessarily what you'll pay**. eBay will bid on your behalf (which is called proxy bidding) by steadily increasing your bid by **small increments until your maximum is reached.**
- **Why?** Because it means **you don't have to monitor the auction** as it unfolds. You also **don't have to worry about being outbid at the very last minute** unless someone bids over your maximum dollar amount. Want more details? Check out an <u>example of proxy bidding</u>.
- **Choose your maximum carefully**, though, as you won't be able to reduce it later.

Your bid is a contract
- Only place a bid if you're serious about buying the item; if you're the winning bidder, you **will** enter into a legally binding contract to purchase the item from the seller.

---

updated listing and see your screen name as high bidder and the current high bid listed at $150. In this case the previous high bidder must have specified a high bid of $145 and when your bid of $225 was entered the previous high bid was surpassed only by the amount determined by eBay™ to be the bid increment for this item (in this case $5). If someone later bids $175 the high bid amount will be raised to match their bid, so you'll now be paying more for the item but you will remain the high bidder. The quilt will eventually be yours unless someone else bids more than $225.

2. You find the same quilt with the same current high bid of $135. This time when you place your bid for $225 you are notified that another bidder has outbid you. What has happened is that the current high bidder, when placing their bid, specified an amount higher than $225. You will now have to raise the amount you are willing to bid if you really want this quilt. After receiving the notice of being outbid you can click the **Back** button on your browser to go back to the bid section and place another bid if you'd like. Just be aware that any time you use the **Back** button to get to a screen where your password was entered you will have to reenter it. It is omitted for security reasons.

Be sure to read Chapter 7—Advanced Tips about the danger of placing a high bid in the hopes nobody else will come close. Never bid more than you are willing to pay, because you just might end up paying close to your top bid.

SELLERS

There are certain fees associated with selling on eBay™ but they are quite a bit lower than your local auction house will charge and you are exposing your merchandise to a much larger audience. Of course you must store the item until sold, and pack and ship it to the buyer. If you're willing and able to do these things, let's sell some stuff!

Establish your account

For convenience and ease of credit approval I recommend you open an account using your credit card during the registration confirmation process. You can also go to the Site Map and register your credit card by clicking **Seller Account-Place or Update My Credit Card**. Your information is taken over a secured line, and I've not heard of anyone in eBay™'s vast user base having problems with billing and/or credit information getting into the wrong hands by submitting it online. Once your card is accepted, it will be used to bill you automatically for any fees you incur each month.

If you don't have a credit card you can still establish an account and be billed monthly, but use the plastic if you have it. You will be billed automatically so you never forget to keep your account current, and you won't be "locked out" from listing an item because your credit limit has been exceeded.

List your item

Click the **Sell Your Item** graphic on the eBay™ homepage. You'll come to a form that you must fill out with your user ID and password, a title for your merchandise, your location (helpful to buyers when calculating postage) and a brief description. Adding photos (covered in depth in Chapter 7—Advanced Tips) is done at this time. You will also have to choose a category in which to place your item, so be sure you've browsed eBay's™ available categories beforehand to have an idea of where your item belongs. You then list the number of items (or groups of items) available in this auction. For instance, if you are selling three glass coasters together it is considered one item. The minimum bid you will accept is entered and if you have a price in mind and won't take less, specify this price as the *reserve*. Reserve protects you in case the bidding is low; you don't have to sell your item unless your reserve price was met. There are then several other options you can select, like making the title of your item bold which makes it stand out more against the others in the category. I recommend not using any of these options unless you know you really have something special for sale, as you pay extra for each one.

One option you should use, which is free, is to select a local region for your listing to be placed in. This is especially helpful when you sell large items that would require great expense to ship. Buyers can browse the listings of sellers within driving distance of them and may place higher bids because of being close enough to pick the item up.

When you have filled in and/or selected all of the necessary items, click **Review** to see a synopsis of the information you've input and a facsimile of your listing. If everything checks out click **Submit My Listing**. A confirmation number will be displayed in your browser window that you should record for future reference, and your item is listed!

Keeping Track of your eBay™ transactions

The easiest and best way to track your activity on eBay™ is to take advantage of a very useful page called simply My eBay™. Each unique registered user has their own My eBay™ page-you can access yours from the **Site Map** link. From here you can monitor every active listing you have posted and the current high bid on it, every item that you have bid on and the current high bid, and the last three feedback transactions someone has posted about you. You can even specify four categories (your favorites) that you can instantly link to from the page. It is a well-designed and extremely helpful addition to the eBay™ community.

Establishing a Sellers Account on eBay™

| Browse | Sell | Services | Search | Help | Community |

Place or update your credit card on your eBay account

Use this secure form to place your credit card on your eBay account or to update your credit card information for automatic payment of your monthly invoice. The transmitted credit card information is protected by the industry standard **_SSL_**.

- Your credit card information will be placed on your eBay account within 24 hours of receipt.
- When you place your credit card on eBay for the **first time**, eBay will attempt to authorize your card. The response from your credit card company will appear on your <u>account status</u> page as either approved or declined. If approved, eBay will bill your credit card each month for your previous month's fees.
- If you already have a credit card on file with us, you can change or update your credit card information at anytime.
- Your credit card will normally be charge 7 to 10 days after receipt of your invoice for the previous mounth's invoice amount.

Click <u>here</u> for more information about eBay Platinum VISA.

1 **STEP 1**
Enter your eBay User ID or email address.

User ID or Email Address	

2 **STEP 2**
Enter your eBay password.

Password	
	(<u>forgotten</u> it?)

3 **STEP 3**
Enter your name exactly as it appears on your credit card.

Your Name	

Establishing a Sellers Account on eBay™ (con't)

STEP 4

Enter your credit card billing address exactly as it appears on your credit card statements. If the address that you enter does not match the address on your credit card statements, your verification will be denied.

Credit Card Billing Address	
	Street
	City
	State/Province
	Zip Code
	United States ▾
	Country

STEP 5

Enter your credit card number.

Credit Card Number	Visa/MC only
	e.g., 4123-4567-8910-1234

STEP 6

Enter the expiration date of your credit card.

Expiration Date	**Month**: `--` ▾ **Day**: `--` ▾ **Year**: `----` ▾
	Leave day as --, if day on credit card is not listed

STEP 7

Click "Submit" to place your credit card information on your eBay account. When you place your credit card on eBay for the **first time**, eBay will attempt to authorize your card. The response from your credit card company will appear on your account status page as either approved or declined. If approved, eBay will bill your credit card each month for your previous month's fees.

Click	Submit

Listing an item for sale on eBay™

ebaY™

Browse | **Sell** | **Services** | **Search** | **Help** | **Community**

sell your item form

▶ Shop with pictures in the **Gallery**.
▶ Learn about **eBay Great Collections**!

[Search field] **Search** tips

☐ Search titles **and** descriptions

Sell Your Item

Related Links: · **New to Selling?** · **Seller Tips** · **Fees** · **Registration**
· **Free Shipping Estimates from iShip.com**

Registration required. You must be a **registered eBay user** to sell your item.

Title required	
	(45 characters max; no HTML tags, asterisks, or quotes, as they interfere with Search) **see tips**

If you prefer to use the old-style method of choosing a category, click **here**.

Category required   You have chosen category # [   ]

Just click in the boxes below from left to right until you have found the appropriate category for your item. The chosen category number will appear in the small box to indicate that you have made a valid selection. Looking for Automotive categories? Choose Miscellaneous : Automotive below.

Antiques ->
Books, Movies, Music ->
Coins & Stamps ->
Collectibles ->
Computers ->
Dolls, Figures ->
Jewelry, Gemstones ->
Photo & Electronics ->
Pottery & Glass ->
Sports Memorabilia ->
Toys, Bean Bag Plush ->
Miscellaneous ->

Description required

You can use basic HTML tags to spruce up your listing. **see tips**

You can add links to additional photos, but enter your primary photo in the Picture

Listing an item for sale on eBay™ (con't)

	URL below. If you want more than one photo for your item, insert its URL in the Description section in the following format: <img src=http://www.anywhere.com/mypicture.jpg>
Picture URL optional	http:// 📷 It's easy! Learn the basics in the <u>tutorial</u>, and enter your URL here.
The Gallery Gallery now has search -- don't let your item get left out! Items in the Gallery get 25% to 200% more bids. <u>learn more</u>	⦿ Do not include my item in the Gallery ○ Add my item to the Gallery (only **$0.25!**) ○ Feature my item in the Gallery (Featured fee of $19.95) http:// If you leave the Gallery URL empty, your Pic URL will be used as your Gallery URL. (Only jpg, bmp, or tif files can be used in the Gallery. Please note that **gif** files will **not** appear in the Gallery!)

Make your item stand out and get more bids! Try these winning options.	
Boldface Title?	☐ $2.00 charge
Featured?	☐ $99.95 charge <u>learn more</u>
Featured in Category?	☐ $14.95 charge <u>learn more</u>
Great Gift icon?	[Not Selected ▾] $1.00 charge <u>learn more</u>

Item location required	[ ] City, State (e.g., San Jose, CA) [Choose the region nearest to you ▾] <u>More about regional selling</u> "Go Local" Regions (US items only) [United States ▾] Country
Payment Methods Choose all that you will accept	☐ Money Order/Cashiers Check ☐ Personal Check ☐ Visa/MasterCard ☐ COD (collect on delivery) ☐ On-line Escrow ☐ American Express ☑ See Item Description ☐ Other ☐ Discover
Where will you ship?	⦿ Ship to Seller's Country Only ○ Will Ship Internationally <u>see tips</u>

Listing an item for sale on eBay™ (con't)

Who pays for shipping?	☐ Seller Pays Shipping ☐ Buyer Pays Fixed Amount ☐ Buyer Pays Actual Shipping Cost ☑ See Item Description

Quantity required	1 If quantity is more than one, then you will have a <u>Dutch auction</u>. <u>see tips</u>
Minimum bid required	_____ per item <u>see tips</u> (e.g., 2.00 -- Please do not include commas or currency symbols, such as $.)
Duration required	7 ▾ days

Reserve Price optional	Enter reserve price **(optional)**: _____ <u>see tips</u> (e.g., 15.00 -- Please do not include commas or currency symbols, such as $.) Careful! Reserve Auction fees will apply **if** your item does not sell (<u>learn more</u>).
Private Auction? optional	☐ Please don't use this unless you have a specific reason. <u>learn more</u>

UserID / Password required	_____ _____ <u>User ID</u> or E-mail address **Password** (<u>forgotten</u> it?)

Press the "review" button below to see what fees are due immediately and what fees may be due if your item sells. You will not incur any fees until you accept the terms disclosed in the next screen.

Press [review] **to review and place your listing.**

Press [clear form] to clear the form and start over.

Note: If the Back button on your browser erases your information on this form, <u>find out</u> how to fix this.

After the Sale

Shortly after the auction ends, you will receive an automatic e-mail message telling you the auction is over, how much the high bid was, and the e-mail address of the high bidder. Have your items packaged and weighed because you will now have to contact the high bidder and inform them of the shipping cost. A small home postage scale is helpful here, but expect to make occasional trips to the post office for accurate costs on larger packages. For help in determining shipping costs for the U.S. Postal Service, refer to Appendix B of this book. You can also get help online at the following Web sites...

U.S. Post Office	**www.usps.gov**
Federal Express	**www.fedex.com**
UPS	**www.ups.com**

Establish policies concerning insurance (I recommend offering it and letting the high bidder decide) and if you will assess a handling charge. You have three days to contact the high bidder with this information and give them a final price (including shipping, insurance, and handling) for the item. Specify payment terms-can you accept credit cards? If so, supply the high bidder with your phone number so that they may contact you with their card number. Most sellers accept personal checks with the condition that the merchandise will be held for a short period of time to allow the check to clear; however some sellers will ship immediately to buyers with high feedback ratings. If the buyer sends you a money order, treat it as cash and ship the merchandise within 24-48 hours.

Keeping Track of your eBay™ Activity

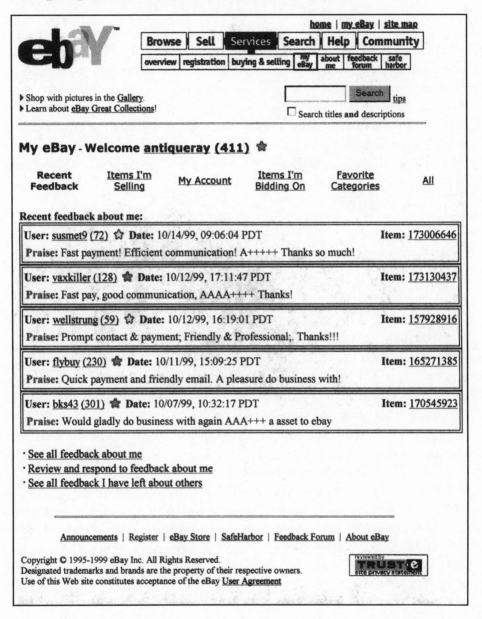

Browse | **Sell** | **Services** | **Search** | **Help** | **Community**

home | my eBay | site map

overview | registration | buying & selling | my eBay | about me | feedback forum | safe harbor

▶ Shop with pictures in the Gallery.
▶ Learn about eBay Great Collections!

Search   tips
☐ Search titles **and** descriptions

My eBay - Welcome antiqueray (411) ✿

Recent Feedback | **Items I'm Selling** | **My Account** | **Items I'm Bidding On** | **Favorite Categories** | **All**

Recent feedback about me:

User: susmet9 (72) ☆ **Date:** 10/14/99, 09:06:04 PDT	Item: 173006646
Praise: Fast payment! Efficient communication! A+++++ Thanks so much!	

User: vaxkiller (128) ✿ **Date:** 10/12/99, 17:11:47 PDT	Item: 173130437
Praise: Fast pay, good communication, AAAA++++ Thanks!	

User: wellstrung (59) ☆ **Date:** 10/12/99, 16:19:01 PDT	Item: 157928916
Praise: Prompt contact & payment; Friendly & Professional;. Thanks!!!	

User: flybuy (230) ✿ **Date:** 10/11/99, 15:09:25 PDT	Item: 165271385
Praise: Quick payment and friendly email. A pleasure do business with!	

User: bks43 (301) ✿ **Date:** 10/07/99, 10:32:17 PDT	Item: 170545923
Praise: Would gladly do business with again AAA+++ a asset to ebay	

· See all feedback about me
· Review and respond to feedback about me
· See all feedback I have left about others

Announcements | Register | eBay Store | SafeHarbor | Feedback Forum | About eBay

CHAPTER 6
The AOL Difference

America Online (AOL) is currently the single most popular Internet Service Provider, though to classify it as such describes but a small part of what it really is. AOL is a community sharing resources like up-to-date news, weather and sports reports as well as online forums where members can interact with celebrities and each other. One of the most popular features is the chat room, where members with like interests can gather, learn, and gossip. There are resources available only to AOL members, and many use AOL for much more than a gateway to the Internet and an e-mail address.

When you choose AOL for Internet access understand that there are a few different rules; while AOL's special features and software mesh with cyberspace, they don't always mesh seamlessly. In this chapter we'll explore some of the differences you'll encounter when using AOL and the online auctions together.

Registering

When registering to buy and sell on eBay™, make sure your mail filters are off or set to accept mail from ebay.com. For more information, go to AOL keyword "mailcontrol" by clicking the "Keyword" button in the upper right corner of your AOL screen.

Bookmarking

AOL users seem to have trouble *bookmarking* eBay™ auctions. Bookmarking is a feature of most browsers that allows you to store the URL of a page for fast and easy return to the same spot later. The problem seems to be that AOL does not save the complete address, which isn't surprising since some of the addresses are quite long. Here is a workaround you can use to successfully bookmark pages from within AOL.

1. From the eBay™ item page click on the Heart icon on the AOL toolbar. A popup menu will prompt you to save to Favorite Places. Click **OK**.
2. Go to **Favorite Places** and highlight the auction item. Click **Modify**.
3. Two dialog boxes will now appear, one containing the Description and the second the Address. In the Address box type at the end of the

address *?item=0000* where 0000 is the item number in the Description box. Click **OK**. The item should now be bookmarked properly for retrieval later.

Posting Photos

After scanning or digitally photographing your item and saving it as a JPEG (.JPG) or GIF (.GIF) file on your computer, you can follow these steps to post the photo from within AOL...

1. Go to Keyword: **MYPLACE**. Reading **My Place Help** will give you an overview of how to upload photos.
2. Click on the box entitled **Go To My Place**
3. Click **Upload**
4. Type the filename of the photo you want to post in the window asking for the remote file name, making sure you type it exactly as it was created including capital and lowercase letters.
5. Be sure **Binary** is selected and click **OK**
6. Click on **Select File**
7. Browse to find the file you want to upload. When you find it, highlight the file and click **OK**
8. Click **Send File**

Let's assume your AOL screen name is **sellme** and you have a photo called **mydoll.jpg** that you want to post on eBay™. After following the above steps, the filename you would use when listing your item on the eBay™ listing form under Picture URL would be **http:// members.aol.com/sellme/mydoll.jpg** and it must be typed exactly to match your screen name and file name, including capitals and lowercase.

CHAPTER 7

Advanced Tips for Online Auction Users

Here are a few tips experience has taught me that will save you some time and trouble. America Online users should refer to Chapter 6—The AOL Difference for instructions on posting photos.

Bidding

So you've tried bidding before reading this chapter? You're probably already acquainted with an online auction fact of life—wanting to be the winning bidder of a particular auction often means you must be at your computer during the last 5-10 minutes watching the bid progress. Many experienced auction goers wait until the last few minutes to bid. During the last two minutes of the auction they often win the item you've been high bidder on for the past six days. This type of bidding is called *sniping* and the people who practice it are referred to as *snipers*.

One remedy to this would be placing a bid so high that nobody else would consider matching it. You might get the item, but often pay more than necessary due to a phenomenon known as *auction frenzy*. Auction frenzy is when several bidders begin to compete in the last few minutes of the auction and throw common sense to the wind—owning the item becomes paramount regardless of price. If you're the unlucky person sitting in the high bidder spot, having bid a foolishly high amount to protect yourself, you may wind up paying a lot more than you bargained for.

If you can't be at your computer when an auction ends for an item you must have, place a bid as high as you are willing to go and hope for the best. If you don't get the item don't despair—quite often another identical or similar and perhaps even better item will come along eventually. Keep watching and use the title search option to locate another example of your must-have item. I've seen three separate items almost identical to each other listed over three consecutive weeks (one week each) by three different sellers on eBay™, each described as rare. Had I wanted to, I could have owned three of the same rare items within a time span of 21 days. Just hang on-you'll find another item to take the place of the one you lost.

Sniping

While we're on the subject of sniping, here's how it's done. When you find an auction item you really want to own, bookmark it and make a note of when the auction is closing. Fifteen minutes before that closing, sit down at your computer, log onto the Internet, find the auction, and get ready to bid the maximum amount you are willing to go. Enter everything just as if you are going to place the bid, but do not click the **Place Bid** bar.

Now launch a new browser window. Simply double-click on the browser icon or do whatever it is you do to open your Internet Explorer, Netscape, or other browser software. A new window will open over top of the one you were just preparing to place your bid in. Adjust the sizes of the windows so that you can view both of them at the same time. This is accomplished in Internet Explorer by placing the cursor over the lower right corner of the window until it turns into a double-headed arrow. You can then click and drag the corner of the windows until they are the size you want them to be.

In the second window you opened, navigate to the auction listing again. Now you have one window showing you the current bid price and time left in the auction and another with the **Place Bid** bar showing. Repeatedly click **Refresh** on the window that shows you the time remaining, clicking at time intervals you are comfortable with, until the clock winds down to less than one minute. Now click on the other window to activate it and immediately click the **Place Bid** bar. Your maximum bid will be recorded.

The potential problem with this method is that if your maximum bid is not high enough to surpass the proxy bid entered by the current high bidder, you won't have enough time left to place another bid if you wanted to. This is why you should just go ahead and place a bid for the maximum amount you are willing to pay—don't try to "nickel and dime" your way into the high bid position.

Of course, there are times when you just can't be at your computer when an auction ends. For instances like this, I recommend you purchase software called Merlin, available for $12.95 from Jason Novak. *Merlin* has an automatic snipe program that will place bids for you while you're away, as well as other tools that make it more convenient to manage your online auction activities. You can find out more about the capabilities of this extremely useful software in my companion book, *The ABCs of Making Money Online*. Order this software by visiting *http://www.pctechzone.com*.

Selling

There are times when it is advantageous to have your item listed in more than one category. Unfortunately, eBay™ does not allow you to do this. Some of the other online auctions do, notably eHammer, for an additional fee. There is a way to duplicate your listing in different categories on eBay™ too, with some extra time and expense, and if you have a desirable item that should be exposed to more than one type of collector I recommend you invest the time and money to do it.

First, submit your listing in the category where you think it fits best, or will be exposed to the most interested bidders. Once the listing is confirmed, visit the auction page and copy the URL of the auction by highlighting it in the browser address window and clicking on **Copy** under your **Edit** menu. You now have a copy of the address of your auction on your computer *clipboard*, and you can duplicate it by selecting Paste, again under the **Edit** menu.

Now return to the Sell Your Item page. Use the same title as you did for your "main" auction, but select a different category this time. When you are doing your description, instead of describing the item you will simply type the following...

<BLOCKQUOTE>**This listing is not active. Please do not place your bid for this item here, as it will not be recognized as a valid bid. If you want to bid on this item, click** <A href="Paste">here </A></BLOCKQUOTE>

Substitute the address you copied to your clipboard for the word "Paste" in the example above, and enclose that address in quotes. Also be sure to use the opening and closing angle brackets just as you see them in the example. Without even trying hard, you've just created an HTML *anchor tag*.

What you are doing is creating a *link* from this page to the actual listing. When the bidder clicks on the word "here" they will be whisked to the auction where bids are being accepted. Now all you have to do is finish filling out any remaining information and submitting the auction. You will end up with two auctions for the same item, one linked to the other. Post a photo in both auctions to pique bidder interest so they are more inclined to click your link to get to the "real" auction.

Of course, you will pay for the second listing. If you start the bidding below $10 with no reserve, you will only pay $0.25 extra. You will also pay the regular eBay™ commission on the high bid achieved by those bidders who will invariably not understand what is going on and place a bid on the wrong auction. There are potential pitfalls with this method, and if you are uncomfortable doing it for any reason, don't. It does work, and if you monitor your auctions and e-mail bidders right away who place bids on the wrong auction to explain what you are doing, misunderstandings can be avoided.

Leave Feedback

You should leave feedback after every transaction, whether you were the buyer or the seller. Feedback helps identify the auction users you should avoid buying from and possibly selling to. Some sellers post in their descriptions that they reserve the right to refuse to sell to users with negative feedback. So it goes without saying you should do everything in your power to keep negatives out of your feedback stable.

Don't be afraid to leave negative feedback for someone who deserves it, but by all means try to settle the situation amicably first. Allow adequate time for the offending party to make good on their promise and e-mail them with non-threatening words of encouragement occasionally. If you've gotten no response for over two weeks, it's time to consider lodging a public complaint via the feedback system. Many people won't do this for fear of retaliation in the form of the offending party leaving negative feedback for them also. Do your duty! Most experienced users understand that one or two negatives surrounded by many more positives means you've been accused unfairly and will give you the benefit of the doubt.

Post a Photo

Using a photo is a must for both buyer and seller, and the photo should be clear and sharp as well as small in file size (50K or less is best). Buyers stay clear of listings without photos because not only can't they pick up the object and examine it, they can't even see it. Even the best description can't always do justice to an object, and a potential buyer doesn't know for sure that the item exists if you haven't displayed a photo of it. Conversely, sellers will realize higher bids for items with photos as opposed to the same item without one. To get a photo posted on the Internet you must have a means of getting the photo into digital form (i.e., digital camera or scanner), an Internet Service Provider that provides some storage capacity on their server (see Chapter 3—Choosing an Internet Service Provider), and software known as *FTP* (file transfer protocol). It's not nearly as daunting as it sounds—let's look closer.

Leaving Feedback after an eBay™ Transaction

eBay™

Browse | Sell | Services | Search | Help | Community

overview | registration | buying & selling | my eBay | about me | feedback forum | safe harbor

▶ Shop with pictures in the Gallery.
▶ Learn about eBay Great Collections!

[Search] tips

☐ Search titles **and** descriptions

Leave Feedback about an eBay User

Your registered User ID

Your password

User ID of person who you are commenting on

Item number (include if you want to relate the comment to a transaction)

You are responsible for your own words.

Your comments will be attributed with your name and the date. eBay cannot take responsibility for the comments you post here, and you should be careful about making comments that could be libelous or slanderous. To be safe, make only factual, emotionless comments. Contact your attorney if you have any doubts. Once left, Feedback **cannot be retracted or edited** by you or by eBay.

Please try to resolve any disputes with the other party before publicly declaring a complaint.

Is your comment positive, negative, or neutral?

○ positive   ○ negative   ○ neutral

Your comment (max. 80 characters)

WARNING: Once placed, comments cannot be retracted. If you later change your mind about someone, you'll have to leave another comment. See the Feedback Forum for an explanation about how your comments affect a users's Feedback Rating.

Click **once** to [leave comment]

Or [clear form] to start again

If you regret a comment you made.
If you have previously left a negative comment and have since been able to resolve your misunderstanding, we encourage you to leave a positive or neutral Feedback comment for that person

If you will be listing items on a limited basis, begin by asking your friends if they know anyone who has a color photo *scanner*. You might be surprised at how many computer users have them in their living rooms and are willing to do some scans for you at a reasonable cost. Your local office supply store may be able to direct you to someone who can do scans on an as-needed basis. But if you plan to do any amount of volume selling, or just plan to be in the online auction game for the long haul, getting your own equipment to post photos on the Internet is a must.

Scanners that can handle color photos, at least at first glance, are the least expensive way to start. Visit any computer superstore or Web site and you'll find color scanners for less than $100. You may want to consider some things before running out and buying one, though. First, it will take practice and patience to learn to use the scanner. While it may not be difficult for the computer-savvy, it's just not as easy as the point-and-click ease of a digital camera. Scanners are also notorious for not interfacing with your computer easily; some require you to get inside the computer case and add new hardware. And while a few of the things you want to scan can be laid directly on the scanner bed, others have to be photographed first anyway due to size, weight, and other considerations. When you photograph with film you have to buy a roll, use the entire roll, take it to be developed, wait for it to be developed, and then scan the photographs. It is neither time nor cost efficient.

If you decide to go the scanner route, most of the flatbed scanners on the market today are adequate for purposes of reproducing a photo of your merchandise. Look for a scanner rated at least 36-bit. The higher the bit rating, the better *dynamic range* the scanner has, meaning it will pick out detail, especially shadow detail, better. Of course with the better dynamic ranges come higher prices. You can get a clear, sharp photo with a 24-bit scanner, but for the slight difference in price go for the higher bit ratings.

Digital cameras have dropped in price drastically since their introduction just a few short years ago. You can now buy a low-end digital camera, which is suitable for most online auction merchandise, at prices not much higher than the 36-bit scanners. It may not pick up the pattern in your Depression glass as well as you'd like, and if you can afford the high-end digital camera for your auction listings you should purchase one. But don't let cost get in the way of having a way of taking digital photos—if you can't afford the best camera buy a low-end one. Many bidders have an extensive library of books that contain photos of the items they are interested in, and these books can show the detail your camera missed.

With the digital camera you simply take the photos and download them via a cable connected from the camera to your computer. Sony makes a very popular camera (Mavica) that stores the photos on a floppy disk that you simply remove from the camera and slide into the floppy drive of your computer. No film to buy. No developing costs. You can take one photo or several. And if you don't like a photo once you see it, you can redo it in minutes. Once you try a digital camera you'll find a lot of alternative uses for it, like e-mailing Sis some photos of your new doll you bought on eBay™.

Whether you decide to go with the scanner or the camera, be sure your purchase includes cables and software to transfer the image from the device to your computer. Some basic image editing software is also necessary that will allow you to brighten dark photos, control the color saturation, and crop the photo to its minimal size. Always crop the photo as small as possible to cut out the background or unimportant elements. The smaller the photo the faster it will load to the browser of a potential bidder.

You must also be able to save the photos in JPEG or GIF format, the two formats used routinely on the Internet. Most scanner and digital camera packages accommodate all of these needs, but you should ask.

After your photo meets your satisfaction and is stored safely on your computer, it's time to transfer it to the space your ISP has provided for you on their server. Most servers require you to use an *FTP* program (Macs use an equivalent called Fetch) that can be downloaded as a free trial from the Internet. Sometimes your ISP will recommend an FTP program and have it available for you to download from their home page, so ask them first. If they have no specific recommendation, two of my favorites are AbsoluteFTP (**www.vandyke.com**) and CuteFTP (**www.cuteftp.com**). Basically the way all FTP programs work is to display two windows, one listing the files on your computer and the other listing the files on your ISP's server. You can move files back and forth from the server and your computer and delete files from either place, which is all you need to be an online auction photo user. FTP programs seem confusing at first, but read the HELP files supplied with them and you'll soon be on your way.

The software needs to know some address information about the server you want to connect to—I recommend you download the FTP of your choice and then call your ISP tech support to get connected. Your ISP can also tell you what URL address to type into your browser window to see your photo once it's uploaded. This will be the same address you use when filling out the online auction form to add a photo. Be sure you use capitals and lowercase EXACTLY as you see it in the filename of your photo. For instance, if you are trying to access a photo called doll.jpg and you type doll.JPG you won't find it!

If you've experimented with FTP and just can't understand exactly how to use it, ask your ISP to walk you through the process while you're sitting at your computer. They may not be familiar with the exact version of FTP you are using, but the mechanics should be very similar no matter what program they have experience with.

Using Multiple Photos with One Listing

There are times when it is necessary to display more than one photo of your item for maximum selling power. This is fairly easy to accomplish.

Instead of using the Picture URL part of the listing form, include the photos as part of the text you write for your listing information. You don't need to understand *HTML* but will need to use it to do this. HTML is hypertext markup language, which is the language of the Internet. Don't be intimidated, all you have to do is follow this example, keying in the codes exactly as here including the opening and closing brackets and slashes. We'll be selling a green Block Optic depression glass bowl and posting two photos (bowl1.jpg and bowl2.jpg) as our example. Remember: you are keying this into the description box. The different typeface in this example denotes HTML coding—you do not actually change typefaces when keying it in.

\<BLOCKQUOTE>This green Depression bowl in the Block Optic pattern is 8.5 inches in diameter. It is in excellent condition with no chips or cracks. Buyer pays $5.00 shipping & handling. Insurance optional. Satisfaction guaranteed.**\</BLOCKQUOTE>**
\<IMG SRC="http://www.yourserver.net/yourscreename/bowl1.jpg">
\<IMG SRC="http://www.yourserver.net/yourscreename/bowl2.jpg">

Adding Multiple Photos on eBay™

	☐ See Item Description
Description (HTML ok)	`<blockquote>This green depression bowl in the Block Optic pattern is 8.5 inches in diameter. It is in excellent condition with no chips or cracks. Buyer pays $5.00 shipping & handling. Insurance optional. Satisfaction guaranteed.</blockquote> <img src=http://www.yourserver.net/yourscreename/bowl1.jpg> <img` (required)
Picture URL	`http://` (optional)
Quantity	`1` (type numerals only) (optional)
Minimum bid	`7.50` per item (numerals and decimal point '.' only) (required) *e.g.: 2.00*
Duration	`7 ▾` days (required)
Reserve price	`22.50` (numerals and decimal point '.' only) (optional) *e.g.: 5.00*
Boldface title?	☐ ($2.00 charge) (optional)
Featured Auction?	☐ ($49.95 charge) (optional)
Featured in Category?	☐ ($9.95 charge) (optional)
Private auction?	☐ Please don't use this unless you have a specific reason. (optional)

Of course you would substitute your own description between the **<BLOCKQUOTE>** and **</BLOCKQUOTE>** codes, and the actual URL of your photos behind the **<IMG SRC**= code. Make sure you use the opening and closing quotes around the URLs. But that's it! It wasn't so hard, was it? Oh, and one more thing. When posting more than one photo, if you want to have the camera icon show up with your listing simply use the Picture URL part of the online listing form for the last photo instead of adding it in your description. In the example above, the bowl2.jpg photo would be dropped from the description and typed in the Picture URL box. Notice that when using the Picture URL box, you do not use brackets like you do when adding photos via the description.

Should you want to add a photo to your listing after your auction is already in progress, most of the online auctions have a link called **Add To Your Item Description** or something similar. Look for it under **Seller Services** on the **Site Map**. You can add photos using the **<IMG SRC**= code exactly as it's shown in the example for adding two photos, again substituting the URL of your pictures.

Adding Multiple Photos on eBay™ to display Camera Icon

	☐ See Item Description
Description (HTML ok)	`<blockquote>This green depression bowl in the Block Optic pattern is 8.5 inches in diameter. It is in excellent condition with no chips or cracks. Buyer pays $5.00 shipping & handling. Insurance optional. Satisfaction guaranteed.</blockquote>` `<img src=http://www.yourserver.net/yourscreename/bowl1.jpg>` (required)
Picture URL	`http://www.yourserver.net/yourscreename/bowl2.` (optional)
Quantity	`1` (type numerals only) (optional)
<u>Minimum bid</u>	`7.50` per item (numerals and decimal point '.' only) (required) *e.g.: 2.00*
Duration	`7 ▾` days (required)
<u>Reserve price</u>	`22.50` (numerals and decimal point '.' only) (optional) *e.g.: 5.00*
Boldface title?	☐ ($2.00 charge) (optional)
Featured Auction?	☐ ($49.95 charge) (optional)
Featured in Category?	☐ ($9.95 charge) (optional)
<u>Private auction?</u>	☐ Please don't use this unless you have a specific reason. (optional)

Start Low

Time and time again it has been proven—you stand a much better chance of your item selling if you start the bidding low. Having no reserve will attract more bidders, as some online auction buyers just won't bid on a reserve auction. They assume that if you set a reserve it is likely high, thereby denying them a bargain.

But no reserve also leaves you open to the possibility of having to sell your item well below market value, and perhaps well below what you paid for it. If you decide to use a reserve, you should start the bidding at roughly 25% of the reserve price. This draws more bidders than if you set the opening bid high with no reserve.

Here's an example. You have an item and you won't sell it for less than $200. Start the bidding at $50 and designate a $200 reserve. When you start the bidding at $200, even if you are selling with no reserve, bidders are reluctant to begin. They might even be willing to pay your price, but would rather have a chance of getting a bargain.

This same mentality is apparent at regular auctions; if you have ever attended one you might have noticed that the auctioneer will first call a price that nobody responds to. He or she might have to drop the starting bid several times before someone will raise their hand, but once it starts, the bidding almost always stops near, and often above, the first price called.

By starting low you will get the interest of more bidders who will then be "watching" your item as the auction progresses. This increases the chances of several people trying to outbid each other for your item in the closing minutes.

Getting Fancy with your Listings

There are several software packages available that make it easy for you to create eye-catching auctions without knowing HTML. Following is an excerpt from my companion book, *The ABCs of Making Money Online* where you will find more complete reviews and information on more similar software packages.

Blackthorne Software Auction Products (http://www.blackthornesw.com)

Blackthorne Software from Sayre, Pennsylvania has developed the definitive software package for listing and tracking your eBay™ auctions. AuctionAssistant is a well integrated group of three different programs consisting of AuctionAssistant2, which includes a great auction formatter called Ad Studio, AuctionTicker, for keeping track of your current auctions, and MegaSets, which gives you the ability to create automatic listings with selected themes. The three programs are sold separately, and AuctionAssistant2 and AuctionTicker can be used independently of each other, but all are designed to work as a group. Let's look at the features of each program individually.

AuctionAssistant2 ($59.95) is a well-designed control panel that allows you to enter your auction information, including up to three photos already stored on your computer. You can browse your hard disk for the photo you want, select it, and AuctionAssistant2 will display the correct file name and show you the actual photo(s) you have selected in a small browser window. You can then automatically upload the photo(s) to your server and post your auction to eBay™. AuctionAssistant2 then becomes a useful archival system that keeps an electronic paper trail to aid you in record keeping.

Another feature of AuctionAssistant2 is the Ad Studio, which allows you to change the colors of your type and backgrounds for your ads. Ad Studio also contains some preset "themes" that use pleasing color combinations and add music to your auctions. There are, including the default theme, a total of 20 different variations included with AuctionAssistant2 version 2.2.

AuctionTicker ($19.95) is an automated program that will log on to the Internet, search for the auction information you want to know about, and then log off. You don't even have to be in the room-your update will be waiting for you when you return. You can choose to have the information displayed in table form, as a scrolling stock-ticker-like form, or both. If you have a soundcard and speakers, you can program AuctionTicker to sound an "alarm" when an auction on your list is about to close (I use the sound of a cash register ringing to remind me it's time to check my bid and possibly bid again). It's a great way to keep from missing out on those must-have items!

MegaSet#1 ($19.95) and/or *MegaSet#2 ($19.95)*, can add even more pizzazz to your auctions! While I usually don't recommend weighing your eBay™ pages down with a lot of bells and whistles, if you're inclined to do so MegaSets allows you to quickly design great ads with themesets like Patriotic, Pythonesque, or 2001 Space Odyssey. There are also holiday themesets for Valentines Day, Halloween, and Christmas. All are complete with backgrounds, colored type, and music, and the files are optimized to take up as little space as possible.

Don't Be A One-Trick Pony

It's easy to follow the crowd and use eBay™ for everything. This book teaches you how to use online auctions using eBay™ as your example, because it is simply the biggest and most well known auction site in existence. But depending on what you are selling, other sites might be better alternatives. For one thing, many other sites do not charge fees for listing items. New sites do this to attract business, and some do it simply to give them a means of competing with eBay™. You are apt to save some money by using some of the smaller sites.

Another thing to consider is that many auction sites tend to become magnets for a certain type of merchandise. If you deal in that type of merchandise you may actually do better on a site that "specializes" in it. On eBay™, the sheer mass of listings makes it hard to be noticed, and unless you have unusual items that stand out in a crowd, you're likely to be lost among the "also-rans".

Title + Description = Sales Pitch

Some people have a way with words. For those who don't, a few basic rules will get you through the writing of your auction description. This is where you put on your sales hat and convince the buying public that your merchandise is worth bidding on.

Stay away from the word "rare" in both your title and description. Rare is the most overused and abused word in the antiques and collectibles industry-most of the items described as rare are not, and items that indeed are rare are not necessarily valuable. Run a search on eBay™ for the word rare to see how many "rare" things are available for sale. Most buyers aren't drawn to listings touting merchandise as rare.

Point out flaws, but gently. Mentioning condition is important, and pointing out the flaws in an item identifies you as an honest seller. But don't dwell on the negative-start out with all of the positive aspects of your item, quickly identify flaws, and end up with more positive comments. It is an established fact that if you get too detailed about the problems of a piece, you will deflate the final bid price of that piece.

Use as many descriptive words and phrases as you can. Do some research before listing if you don't know anything about the item. Often you can find a similar item by searching the eBay™ completed auctions-you can then glean information from the descriptions of others. The more details you provide the better chance you have of attracting the bidders that will drive up the price. Here's an example-which of the following titles are more likely to attract bidders?

Wood Stand
19th century mahogany candle stand with spoon carving

A fold-out photo book
of New York City
scenes taken in 1875.

A Chronometer manufactured
by Hamilton Watch Company
of Lancaster, PA.

CHAPTER 8

Protecting Yourself from Internet Auction Fraud

A sad fact of life is that as long as online venues exist for people to buy and sell, con artists and hucksters will likely know about them. Internet auctions provide just such a venue-one that is largely unregulated. The better online auctions have taken some steps to protect your privacy and security, but when fraud occurs it comes down to the fact that you are on your own to protect yourself. Most of these sites exist simply to match buyer and seller, and the auction assumes no liability beyond that.

Online auction fraud, while not prolific, is real enough to have prompted the Federal Trade Commission to call a meeting with the top Internet auction sites in May 1998. While the cause may have been admirable, the auction representatives were not optimistic about the prospects of a successful plan to cut back on fraud. Even legally defining fraud becomes an issue; there exists a fine line between proving the seller was willfully deceiving the buyer and the buyer's failure to ask enough questions before bidding. We probably all have a different opinion of what constitutes "very good" condition, and other such generic terms. As with transactions you make in your everyday life the common sense approach seems to be "buyer beware."

While there is no failsafe way to be sure you're dealing with a reputable buyer or seller, there are some steps you can take to greatly reduce your risk.

BUYER'S REMEDIES

√ Read the description twice

Reading a description the first time through most people will have a mental image of the item, as they would like it to be. The second time reality begins to set in. And for some of us it takes a third and fourth read before we really get the picture. The extra time is worth it-the most common complaint from online auction buyers is that the merchandise was not as described. This can also mean the buyer did not interpret the description as the seller intended.

√ E-mail sellers with questions

Descriptions of merchandise being sold via online auctions vary from highly detailed to unbelievably incoherent. Even the highly detailed ones probably won't answer every question you should ask the seller. Clarifications on condition, color, manufacturer's marks and size or dimensions are sometimes necessary—although photos are an extremely important aid to the description they can be deceiving. More importantly, two questions that are almost never answered in the description should be the first ones you ask: seller's return policy (covered next) and shipping charges. Almost invariably the seller will mention in the description "Buyer pays shipping," which is normal and fair for online auctions. But how much shipping? Some will send your package for the actual cost of postage. Others charge a handling fee and I've seen them range from $0.25 to $5 for handling on a small object alone. Sellers are entitled to a handling fee to cover expenses of packing materials and their time. But some are using the handling fee as a profit extender and you should know before you buy how much you'll be charged. If it seems exorbitant, don't bid.

√ Know the seller's return policy

Make sure you understand the seller's return policy, especially if you're bidding on a high-ticket item. Most don't mention their policy so be sure to inquire before you bid. Buyers remorse is never an excuse to return an item, but if you feel strongly that the merchandise is not what was described you should know your options.

I've seen sellers who absolutely refuse to accept returned items. Some charge restocking fees designed to make it cost-prohibitive to return things, and some will honor legitimate returns as long as you are willing to pay their cost of running that particular auction and/or shipping charges to return the item. My advice is simply this: *don't bid on an auction where the seller has a no return policy*. I don't buy from antique malls or retailers advertising a no return policy and online sellers are no different.

√ Insure your purchases

Still another consideration is whether or not the item will be insured; some sellers require you to pay for insurance while others let you decide or never mention it at all. Any item you are willing to pay your hard-earned money for is worth insuring, especially breakables. Requesting insurance lets the seller know you are a serious buyer and as such won't be as quick to tolerate inferior merchandise or service. In my dealings with shipping online auction merchandise I have not had a single package lost in the mail in over 300 shipments; however there has been breakage reported eight times. I deal primarily with the U.S. Postal Service and except for one case all claims have been fully paid promptly and courteously. The one "problem" case involved a buyer living on a U.S. military installation. The buyer was asked to fill out forms that were then mailed to the seller (me). I had to fill out the seller's part and mail them somewhere else for verification. Sadly the buyer e-mailed me two months after I had returned the forms to let me know they still had not heard a thing about their claim. I don't know if the difference in the refund procedure was due to the APO address or not, but it may be something buyers living on military bases should be aware of.

The U.S. Postal Service charges a small fee for insurance which is well worth the expense; you will find this schedule of fees in Appendix B. UPS will insure packages with a declared valued up to $100 for no extra charge. Higher amounts can be purchased at a cost of $0.35 for each $100 of declared value over $100, with a maximum of $50,000. Federal Express also gives you the first $100 of declared value at no extra charge, and then charges a minimum of $2.50 for insurance up to $500. Above that the charge is $0.50 for each $100 increment or fraction thereof.

√ Can you see it?

Photos of merchandise being offered are common when using the larger online auctions and infinitely helpful in making buying decisions. How often have you bought something from a retail store or catalog without seeing at least a picture? Most of you wouldn't do such a thing, and you shouldn't buy something online unless there is a photo of it posted.

Some sellers don't post a photo but offer to e-mail one if you request it. This is fine, and you should by all means request the photo if you're interested in what they have to offer. Once you've seen it you know it exists, and many of us are better equipped to make decisions based on sight rather than reading a description.

There are enough options available to today's online sellers—ranging from low-cost digital cameras and scanners to photo studios that can convert images to Internet formats—that there just isn't an excuse for not having a photo available for a prospective buyer. For information on how to post your pictures once you have them digitized, see chapter 7—Advanced Tips for Online Auction Users.

√ Read the feedback

Most online auctions provide the ability for registered auction-goers to leave feedback for buyers or sellers they've had dealings with. You can leave positive, negative, or neutral comments and the results are posted and available to anyone requesting the information. Before bidding on merchandise from a seller you aren't familiar with, read their feedback profile. There should be few, if any, negative comments.

If there are one or two negatives posted, e-mail the person(s) who left them (e-mail addresses are usually available with the feedback summary) and ask for details. Most online auction users are happy to talk about their experiences, good or bad. Don't rule out someone with a negative or two if there are many positives—perhaps the comment was unfair or unwarranted or the matter could have been amicably resolved had the offended party been more patient.

√ Return when not as described

When you accept merchandise that is not what the seller described, you are contributing to the stereotype of antique dealers being dishonest. My personal experiences, both online and off, is that the vast majority of antique and collectible dealers are honest and concerned about the reputation of the industry. If you find one that isn't, letting them get away with it encourages unacceptable behavior.

Since you've already determined you are dealing with someone having an acceptable return policy (you have done that, haven't you?), by returning the item you're saying, "I don't accept inferior merchandise." Of course, reread the description before contacting the seller and make sure your expectations weren't too high. If they were, accept your mistake and leave positive feedback for the seller. If you're still sure you didn't get what was described, make contact and explain your reasons for the return.

√ Add your 2 cents

It's been mentioned before but it's worth mentioning again: after completing your transactions, make sure you post feedback about the other party. Don't be shy if you've been ripped off—some people won't post negative feedback about someone else for fear of retaliation and receiving negative feedback themselves. While this can't be ruled out, astute online auction users know that some negatives are unwarranted and won't hold them against you, especially when the vast majority of your feedback is glowing. An undeserved negative may hurt your pride, but you've done the auction community a service by exposing a con artist. And leaving feedback is like voting: if you don't do it you have no reason to complain when the system doesn't suit you.

√ Visit chat rooms

Some of the online auctions have chat rooms where buyers and sellers gather to talk about their experiences. You can gain valuable auction tips here as well as learn about particular users who have abused the system.

SELLER'S REMEDIES

√ Nonpayment

Buyer's remorse is a part of this business you'll probably have to deal with at some point if you sell long enough. Be sure you make every effort to solve the situation amicably first but when the buyer doesn't pay up and offers no reasons after two weeks, post negative feedback. The fee to list your item is probably nonrefundable, but many of the online auctions will credit your account for the commission charge if you ask. Make sure you ask. And add this buyer to your no-repeat-business list.

√ Item switching

A few unscrupulous buyers are upgrading their collections by making a purchase, claiming a defect with the merchandise, and returning an identical item of lesser quality, sometimes even damaged. The only way I can suggest to combat this scam is to photograph your item before you ship it and store the photo with documentation about the condition. Of course I wouldn't do it for everything, but you know which pieces you need to protect.

BENEFICIAL TO BOTH BUYER AND SELLER

√ Escrow Companies

Many of the online auctions are beginning to promote the services of a third party escrow company to act as a go-between for buyer and seller. The escrow companies benefit both parties—buyers are protected from fraudulent merchandise and sellers get protection from buyers who don't pay. Money from the buyer is sent to the escrow company, who holds it in trust until the merchandise is delivered and accepted. The escrow company then releases the buyer's funds to the seller. Should the merchandise not be as described or never delivered, the money is not yet in the seller's hands. Conversely, if the buyer does not pay, the seller never has to ship the merchandise.

√ Online Help

eBay™ has an area of their community set aside for help and protection with online transactions. It is called SafeHarbor™ and includes links to the eBay™ help desk, the tutorial, an Escrow Company, and other useful information.

Information from other sources is also available online about protecting yourself from fraud when using the Internet. The Federal Trade Commission maintains a site (www.ftc.gov) with consumer information that applies to Internet shopping in general, not just auctions. From their home page click on Consumer Protection and then on E-commerce and the Internet for a list of topics.

If you follow the recommendations outlined in this chapter and still become a victim of fraud, you do have other options. The National Fraud Information Center in March of 1996 launched the Internet Fraud Watch, enabling them to expand their responsibilities to this area of commerce. Electronic forms are available to report fraudulent practices or request information. You can reach the Internet Fraud Watch at www.fraud.org or by calling 1-800-876-7060.

If you buy from a business and get ripped off, you can go to www.bbb.org and also file a complaint with the Better Business Bureau. You might as well make noise with as many third party enforcement organizations as you can—after all, it's your money!

A Delft Toby jug reputed to date from the 18th century. Delft, Majolica and Faience are all relatively numerous online.

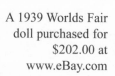

A 1939 Worlds Fair doll purchased for $202.00 at www.eBay.com

A 23 inch
Shirley Temple doll,
sold on eBay™.

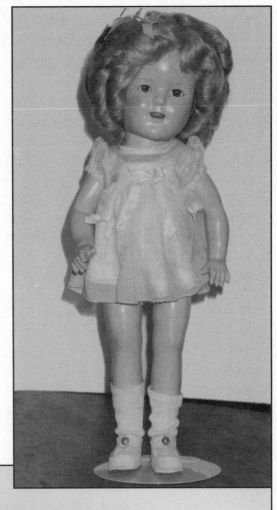

Automotive collectibles are
well represented on the
Internet.

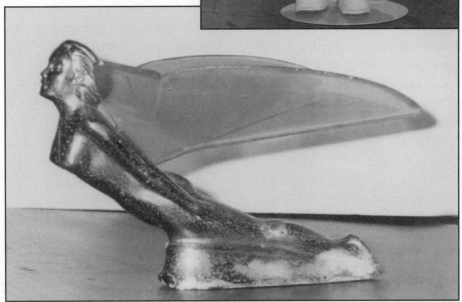

Epilogue
Buyer Beware!

Although you are exposed to hundreds, perhaps thousands, of objects to collect on the Net, the variety is counterbalanced by the possibility that the items aren't necessarily described in the terms and with the accuracy you would wish. This may be because the person selling the item is not knowledgeable about this particular kind of collectible. When you see terms misused, it should be a signal to you to inquire further about the object.

Another warning signal is when the photograph of the object you are interested in is too fuzzy to clearly show details. Perhaps the seller is just a bad photographer, but unless you can clearly see the item in the photograph, it is wise to steer clear or at least request another picture before bidding.

It is not at all unusual for an item to be listed in the wrong category. "Antique Dolls" is a category that covers a lot of territory, but dolls like a 1967 Eegee doll, a *Crissy* doll, or a Precious Moments nativity set, all of which are listed as "antiques" as this is written, do not belong in that category!

As a doll collector, I am often puzzled and sometimes amused at the descriptions given for dolls. At the moment a "15 inch German Schoenhut Doll" is listed with references to Jan Foulke's *Blue Book of Dolls and Values* and Coleman's *The Collector's Encyclopedia of Dolls*. How would someone with access to those two excellent reference books make such a basic mistake as to call a Schoenhut a German doll? Right away that seller loses credibility.

I am always wary of the term "rare" used in a description. Perhaps this is just a way to entice buyers to look at a particular selection, but it is misused in the vast majority of cases. "Very rare," "very old," and "early" are also often misused. As this is written there is a "Rare German paper (sic) mache, ca 1880" listed. It appears to be a nice doll, but rare she is not! An "Early 1800's Wax Doll—Rare" is also interesting, but the photograph indicates that she is a wax-over composition with pierced ears that dates from the last quarter of the 19th century, so I have a problem with the use of both "rare" and "early" in that description.

Recently a doll was advertised as a "bisque head" "Holtzmasse." Curious because it could only be one or the other but not both, I found out that it was a bisque head doll by Cuno & Otto Dressel—the firm that held the trademark for "Holtzmasse." Holtzmasse is a word for a wood-pulp composition material so it was stamped on their papier-mâché dolls but never on their bisque ones. So it is still a puzzle—"Holtzmasse" is nowhere on the doll (nor should it be) but indicates some knowledge of the COD dolls. However, why would a seller pick up that term "out of the air" and use (or misuse) it to describe a bisque doll?

Carolyn Cook

Baby boomers can find childhood memories
available for sale online.

APPENDIX A—Glossary

Alta Vista—one of the major search engines on the World Wide Web.

America Online—an online community of member services and gateway to the Internet.

auction frenzy—the madness that sometimes prevails in the last few minutes of an online auction as bidders try to outbid each other.

bookmarking—storing the Internet addresses of your favorite Web sites for fast retrieval later.

browser—software that enables your computer to translate and display Web pages on your computer monitor.

CD ROM—Compact Disk, Read Only Memory. The disk looks like a typical music CD and holds data to install programs or run games on your computer.

clicking—the act of pressing one of the buttons on your computer mouse.

Control Panel—an area of your computer accessible from the Start—Settings menu.

copy & paste—two separate functions that allows you to make a copy of some data and place it in another file. Usually found under the Edit menu of your word processing program.

crop—electronically "trimming away" any extraneous parts of a photograph, leaving only as much of the image as is necessary to show off your item. The photo manipulation software that comes with most scanners or digital cameras allows you to do this.

Earthlink—a national Internet Service Provider.

encryption—a method of "coding" information sent via e-mail to make it much more difficult for anyone, other than the recipient, to be able to intercept and interpret it.

flaming—the online equivalent of vehemently criticizing someone, sometimes nastily.

frames—a construction technique used by some Web site designers that utilizes two or more windows open at the same time. Some older browsers cannot interpret frames.

FTP—file transfer protocol. Software that enables you move files between your ISP's server and your computer.

http—hypertext transfer protocol. The rules used to create Web pages, enabling users to transfer hypertext and multimedia from one networked computer to another.

hyperlink—word(s) or photo(s) on a Web page that, when clicked, take you to another area of the World Wide Web.

iMac—the first new computer introduction by Macintosh in years. Designed to compete with the PC in the under $1,500.00 consumer computer market.

ISDN—Integrated Services Digital Network. A series of standards for transmission over ordinary telephone lines at up to 128 Kbps. Typically costs $400-$500 for installation and $20 monthly over and above your regular phone charges.

ISP—Internet Service Provider. A business that provides Internet access to the public.

Keywords—descriptive word(s) and phrases used to instruct other software, often search engines, to perform certain tasks.

Launch—the act of initiating a program on your computer.

Linking—the ability, through the use of hypertext transfer protocol, to move from one part of the World Wide Web to another.

Macintosh—a computer that competes with the PC and runs a completely different operating system.

megahertz—a unit of measurement (one million cycles of electromagnetic currency alternation per second) used to rate the speed of computer microprocessors. The higher the megahertz rating, the faster the computer microprocessor can interpret information.

Modem—Hardware that enables two networked computers to transfer data back and forth.

newsgroup—an online group formed to discuss one particular topic.

PC—Personal Computer. IBM built the first PCs but today the market is dominated by PC clones built by other manufacturers.

Point your browser—instructing your browser software as to its next destination.

RAM—Random Access Memory. Hardware which stores important data for running your computer. The more RAM your computer has the faster most applications will run.

reserve—the minimum amount of money you are willing to accept for your item.

robot—a program that automatically scans the Web and retrieves HTML documents to be indexed and stored for later retrieval.

Search engine—a powerful program that enables you to locate specific information on the World Wide Web by typing in descriptive words.

sniper—an online auction participant who waits until the last minutes of an online auction and then places a high bid with little time left for others to outbid them.

sniping—the act of waiting until the last minutes of an online auction to place your bid with the intent of leaving other bidders no time to outbid you.

Storefront Auction—an online auction that is actually a retail Web site in disguise.

T-1 Line—a direct connection to the Internet using fiber optic cabling with speeds of up to 192 Kbps.

URL—Uniform Resource Locator. An Internet address that you type in to access a Web page. Each Web page has a unique URL so that it can be individually accessed by anyone online.

Usenet—newsgroups when referred to collectively rather than indivdually.

Web page—all of the text, graphics, audio and video that your browser displays when you type in an Internet address, or URL.

Web site—a series of Web pages on a common topic that are linked together using hyperlinks.

WebTV—a device, similar in looks to a cable TV box, which enables the user to connect to the Internet without a computer.

Yahoo—one of the major search engines on the World Wide Web.

APPENDIX B—U.S. Postal Service Rate Charts

These rates are taken from the United States Postal Service Web site (**www.USPS.gov**) and reflect rates that went into effect on January 10, 1999.

Priority Mail

Up to 2 pounds	$3.20
Up to 3 pounds	$4.30
Up to 4 pounds	$5.40
Up to 5 pounds	$6.50

Over 5 pounds the rates change according to distance shipped. For best accuracy take packed item to your local post office with the zip code of recipient, or visit **www.usps.gov** to calculate cost.

First-Class Mail

1 ounce	$0.33
2 ounces	$0.55
3 ounces	$0.77
4 ounces	$0.99
5 ounces	$1.21
6 ounces	$1.43
7 ounces	$1.65
8 ounces	$1.87
9 ounces	$2.09
10 ounces	$2.31
11 ounces	$2.53
12 ounces	$2.75
13 ounces	$2.97

Over 13 ounces see Priority Mail

Insurance

Coverage is based on amount of insured value. Do not insure a package for more than its value.

Insured Value	Fee
$0.01-$50.00	$0.85
$50.00-$100.00	$1.80
$100.01-$200.00	$2.75
$200.01-$300.00	$3.70
$300.01-$400.00	$4.65
$400.01-$500.00	$5.60
$500.01-$600.00	$6.55
$600.01-$700.00	$7.50
$700.01-$800.00	$8.45
$800.01-$900.00	$9.40
$900.01-$1,000.00	$10.35
$1,000.01-$5,000.00	$10.35

Additional insurance is $0.95 for each $100.00 or fraction thereof over $1,000.00.

Insured mail maximum liability: $5,000.00

INDEX